The Athlete's Guide to Sponsorship

*An Athlete Entrepreneur's Guide to Dreaming Big, Racing Smart
& Creating a Reliable Brand for a Long, Successful Career*

For all of the athletes that I've worked with over the years, thanks for the inspiration, the perspiration, and the dedication.

Table of Contents

BUSINESS OF FITNESS

Introduction

So you want to be a pro athlete? Awesome. But … How do you do it?

You put in the training hours, you start doing well at races, and then a big team or company just hands you a suitcase full of money, right?

Cue sad trombone music.

Sadly, it's not quite that simple. There are thousands of amazing athletes all over the world who can't make a living at their sport. Even Olympic medalists often aren't bringing home enough cash to pay the rent, if they're only relying on what the national team can provide. By the time you shell out cash for the gear, the race entries, the travel, the lodging, the food, the massages, the gear you need after you break or wear out the first set… It's freaking expensive to be a pro.

You can dream of the day when a team sends that invite with a hefty salary, or the sponsor reaches out and wants to give you a big check instead oft a box of almost-expired gels. But the times are changing for racers, and as fitness 'influencers' take over some of the space that used to be occupied by you, the endurance athlete, you're going to have to do more than just score some decent results. You don't need to be Insta-famous to make a living in endurance sports like running, cycling, or triathlon, or in solo adventure sports like rock climbing. But you will need to do more than just your sport: You're going to have to learn to market yourself in a smart, authentic, deliberate way.

Fortunately, you're not the first person who's had to figure this out. As the landscape of the athletic world changes, there are plenty of badass athletes who've learned to change with the times, while retaining their individual brands and not losing training hours or integrity in the process.

This book is filled with tips and tricks from them, as well as from sponsorship coordinators, team directors and many more industry experts. Not every chapter will apply to you, but if you're looking to find your way onto a team, improve your status with your current sponsors while seeking out new ones, or simply be the most marketable athlete that you can be, keep reading.

I've seen dozens of careers made, and seen athletes with great results opting to leave the sport, defeated. While raw talent is important, what I've come to realize is that there's so much more to finding and keeping a sponsor, and that's a concept that many athletes are unaware of, or simply don't understand. Endurance sports—like cycling, running or triathlon—are a unique when it comes to sponsorship: they rely heavily on personality as well as power output, and results on their own don't dictate livelihoods.

From the influencer side of things, I've made friends with some of the biggest in the business, I've seen a best friend rise to influencer status seemingly by accident. I've also seen some get cut down and lose partners and sponsors. Going through yoga teacher training, I shared a space with a dozen wannabe influencers, some of whom are making it, and some who've re-joined the 9 to 5 workforce. Because frankly, being an influencer, like being a pro athlete, is f***ing hard. It's a job, just like any office one, but it's more personal, it's more dependent on you being you—there's no faking it.

And let's be honest, at this point, the differences between fitness influencers and athletes are shrinking: Lots of sponsorship dollars are being determined by social reach in addition to race results. At the end of the day, for most companies, it's about who can help them sell the most product.

And even when you think you've got it made—you sign one big deal, land a huge sponsor—it only lasts as long as the terms on your contract, and then you're back to the negotiating table.

I'll be blunt: This life you're choosing? You probably won't get rich. But if you can develop routines, systems and plans around the 'care and keeping' of sponsors and partners, you're more likely to be able to have a steady career as an athlete.

Many athletes don't understand how the sponsorship systems work, or just don't understand how to go about finding the right person to talk to at the right time. Those who do figure out how to play the game, they are the select few who truly make it in the sport. You might make it to a road team, you might make it onto a mountain bike program based solely on your ability to pedal really, really fast, but to thrive in the industry, to secure independent sponsorships that take you from making a salary to really making a living, and to have a career waiting for you when you do retire, you need to not just be fast, you need to be a highly-sponsorable athlete.

And in today's world of social media and online marketing, new blogs and magazines and podcasts popping up weekly, plus the traditional model of meet-and-greets, races and clinics, it can be a minefield. Even applying to teams or hunting down new sponsors can be tricky: does a fantastic race resume matter as much as decent results plus a huge social media following? The answer, of course, is: It depends. (This is going to be a theme.) But there are ways to increase your sale-ability, especially for young athletes hoping to secure spots on development teams, or solo riders hunting for one-off sponsorships.

That means you need to hustle and find a team that can actually pay you living wage, figure out a job that you can work while pursuing your sport, or cobble together enough sponsorships to keep you afloat.

Consider this tale of two racers: one, shy by nature and stubborn to a fault, raced to his last Nationals win on a bike with the logos taped over and a sponsorship slapped together at the last second by family friends. The next season, despite being a current National Champion, he struggled to find a solid program for the season. The other racer, by contrast, won Nationals the next year while being fully supported by his team, and his win was commemorated on his wildly popular Internet reality show. The results were exactly the same— Nationals wins—but the payoff for racer 1 was five figures, while racer 2 was bringing in multiple six-figure deals with the same race results.

Both racers have managed to keep their careers going, and support their families while doing it. But for the vivacious, extroverted Racer #2, the art of the sponsor hustle came a little bit easier, and it showed—even to people who weren't on the inside.

Moral of the story? It isn't always about the results; it's about the racer. The purpose of this workbook is to educate you as you begin trying to take your careers to the next level, whether you're a junior looking for a developmental team, or mom of two who's discovered cycling and started winning races left and right. We'll talk about how to find sponsors and teams, and once found, how to keep them.

"It's kind of a bummer when you just want to ride your bike, since that's a full-time job without considering the business side of it," one sponsorship coordinator told me. He's fielded thousands of resumes from riders who had plenty of talent, but none of the spark that he was looking for. And he's gotten to work with some of the best—and the worst—in the business.

Not a cyclist? This book works for any endurance sport, from running to triathlon to the fast-growing sport of obstacle course racing. If the traditional team model (think NFL) isn't prevalent in your sport, you'll learn something from this.

So who am I, and why did I think I could write this book? While I've never 'made it' in the pro ranks, I've had an even better education in the industry, working inside it and helping choose new team members, balance sponsorship budgets, interview pro racers and coach training camps. I've raced my bike at the elite level while writing about every kind of racer for dozens of major publications, coaching junior elite training camps, and living in communities all over North America in houses of athletes devoted to making it as pros. I've managed one of the biggest cyclocross programs in the world, and traveled all over North America and Europe to do it. From junior development teams, to struggling mid-twenties racers, to the multi-time National Champion, to road teams who appear "pro" but are still camping in basements as they tour the country racing, I've seen how important the role of sponsorship is.

This book was inspired both by what I saw working for racers, and what I saw other racers with similar results missing in their search for a decent livelihood. I've spent a lot of time coaching camps with junior racers, and have a fantastic track record when it comes to predicting which riders will make it onto pro teams and which will leave the sport within a few years—not because of results, but because of an inability to turn a passion into a career.

Do I think everyone needs to have a booming social media presence and a kickass website? Not necessarily. Will it hurt your career to try to be more marketable? Absolutely not. So what do you have to lose?

Ask yourself: what do you want from your athletic career? If the answer is more than Ramen noodles for dinner and a couple good results, read on.

Before you dive in: I'd recommend grabbing some kind of journal and pen or having your laptop on hand, since I include plenty of quick journaling exercises that you can do to think about new and interesting ways to look at sponsorship. I'd also recommend starting a spreadsheet in Excel or Google Sheets labeled SPONSORSHIP, because there are quite a few spots in here where creating a table is going to be super helpful.

A final note: People interviewed for this book are often anonymous to protect the innocent (and the guilty). You'll see why. But understand that everything in here is 100 percent true to life.

GETTING STARTED

The Golden Rule

Still reading? Awesome. So, let's talk about the big rule that covers almost every part of this book. Remember that thing your parents used to tell you? You know, the Golden Rule: "Do to others what you want them to do to you."

Basically? Don't be a dick.

Everyone that you meet from this point on is a potential teammate, sponsor, friend or fan. The less enemies you make—in the race and after the race—the better your chances are of success. The more people you're nice to, the more fans you win over to your side, the better your career will go.

There are very few athletes who are good enough at their sport that their bad behavior is excused. For 99.9 percent of athletes, an ill-timed temper tantrum is enough to not get your contract renewed. (And if you're reading this book, you're almost certainly in that 99.9 percent of the population.)

Sure, there are some guys and girls—who shall remain nameless—that find success in spite of (or even partially because of) their bad attitudes. You don't want that to be you, because even if those racers are making it right now, it's not likely to last. Those are the racers who, as soon as they're not getting results, or the tide of social media turns against them, are losing contracts and not getting jobs afterwards.

And furthermore, you don't really want to be a jerk, do you?

So, let's just nip this one in the bud: be nice to people. Be nice in person, be nice on the internet, be nice on the phone. Just. Be. Nice.

It's that easy—and yet, this is so often the big thing that's missed. If you take nothing else from this book, take that. Almost everything else stems from that simple point.

Got it? OK, let's move on.

Don't Quit Your Day Job (Yet)

We're going to start with the cold, hard truth. Sorry about this, but here goes: Being a professional athlete is hard, especially when it's your day job and not just a passion or hobby. Before you read any further, it's worth pausing and reflecting for a few minutes as to whether this is something you really do want to pursue as a career versus the thing that you do for fun (and maybe a bit of profit!) on the weekends.

This is a struggle I've had over the years, and one that I've watched a lot of other racers go through. Even ones with all the talent in the world, who show that 'glimmer' that they might just be able to be great, might not be willing to put in the immense sacrifices that go with it. And that's OK: For instance, I find that writing about it while being a decent racer on the side (and being able to hop into any race I feel like, whether it's a marathon or a road stage race) is what I really wanted. It might take some trial and error to figure that out. In fact, it probably will.

The good news? You can race at the highest of levels while holding down another career—in fact, most racers do. Even OCR champion-turned-ultrarunner Amelia Boone was working full-time when she was at her peak. Endurance sports tend to be different than your typical Big-5 sports—multimillion dollar contracts are hard to come by. Even rockstar climber Alex Honnold isn't making bank: watch Free Solo and listen to him tell a class of kids that he makes about as much as a dentist or doctor does. Expect a lot of years of hustle and serious racing while maintaining other income streams before you're ever existing solely on sponsorship dollars.

And then, when you do make it, you're still never going to be just training and racing. At the highest level, being a sponsored athlete is essentially a full-time job outside of the actual training and racing part, between web and social updates, sponsor obligations, contract negotiations, money management, balancing your race schedule with your training, connecting with fans at races, et cetera.

As you're getting started—at whatever age you are when you're reading this—you might not have any other job or you might be working a 40 hour workweek at an office. Actually, on average, the most successful athletes I know are the ones who have a day job, whether it's working for a law firm, teaching full-time, or even being a part-time mechanic at a local bike shop. Those are the athletes who aren't constantly plagued by training thoughts, overtraining issues, and overthinking what's going on with their sport.

For younger racers, this might look like going to school. Or it might mean a part-time job on top of school during the summer.

As we'll get into in later chapters, having an outside source of income is a serious plus: It can make racing successfully a lot easier because it means you can afford things like clean, healthy food; you can pay for a hotel instead of sleeping in your car at a race; and you aren't reliant on begging sponsors for the little stuff like socks and drink mix. Not stressing about where your next paycheck comes from can be just as valuable as 20 extra hours a week to train, sleep or recover… And being able to buy quality groceries and turn on the air conditioning without worrying about the utilities bill is worth a bit less time to prop your legs up post-run.

Keeping a day job also forces you to really make the choice to be a pro, and appreciate what it means. It's easy to train like a pro when you're living with your parents and don't need to pay any bills. But the pro racers who I've seen succeed and crush it in races and with their sponsors are the ones who've had to struggle, who've had to work part-time jobs as programmers or janitors in order to fund their racing habit at the beginning. Those are the ones with the true grit, the ones who will be standing on the next start line when you've hopped on the plane to go back to your parent's house after a race didn't go your way.

That's harsh, but that's the reality you're facing.

So, two morals here:

First: You most likely haven't chosen a super-lucrative career. Maybe eventually, you'll make good money just for racing, but you'll be lucky to make as much as a doctor or a lawyer. That means you need to know that being a pro racer is something that you really, truly want to do. You could be a manager at a coffeeshop and probably make as much (or more) as you'll make for the first decade of racing, and still be able to race on the weekends for fun. There's nothing wrong with that: You can still race at a pretty high level more for the enjoyment, maybe pick up a couple small sponsors or ride for a fun local team. You have to really, really want it if you think this is honestly the career you want to pursue.

Second: Even if you do decide that being a pro athlete is your career path, there's nothing wrong—and everything right—with having some kind of side gig, full or part-time. You'll be much more prepared to be a solid, well-rounded athlete who helps lead the team, versus a young racer who's only ever relied on a parent or allowance as his or her method of support.

Figuring Out Your Niche

As an amateur athlete, you can get away with racing a lot of different disciplines. In fact, most racers start out in multiple disciplines, maybe racing road, mountain bike, gravel, and cyclocross. Or a runner might jump into 5Ks and marathons, maybe dabbling in cross-country. That's great, if you just want to enjoy racing.

But if you actually want to make it in your field, you need to figure out what your niche is, and stick to it. For example, a strong road racer may be doing OK on a team as a domestic rider, but might be able to rock a gravel grinder and come out on top in most races. That means it's either time to double down on road training to be better than just OK on the circuit, or it might mean changing allegiances and focusing on finding solo sponsors for a career as a gravel grinding badass.

Early in your career, you might be able to handle balancing a few different disciplines, and you might even be able to hop into a couple of non-niche races as training—a lot of cyclocross racers, for example, will race road or mountain bikes in the summer in order to prep for their seasons. But know exactly why you're doing any of those races, and make sure that they make sense within your bigger plans.

Don't race a second season at the expense of your primary season, don't risk burnout for results that ultimately won't matter to a team or a sponsor. (For instance, if you're a marathon runner, it doesn't make sense to jump into a mountain bike race, no matter how fun it sounds.)

Step one: Figure out what you want to be known for.
Step two: Become known for it.

If you don't know what your niche is right now, don't worry—a lot of the exercises in this book are designed to help you move closer to figuring it out, but you can start by thinking through where you've had your best results and where you've had the most fun racing. Often, your niche is at the intersection of those two things.

Influencer vs. Athlete

This is a tricky distinction and it can make a difference in terms of your approach with potential partners/sponsors. The distinctions between athlete and influencer are becoming less and less, but there are a few. It's worth understanding this because there are some of you reading this who may realize that you actually fit slightly better into the influencer model when it comes to seeking sponsorships and partners.

An athlete can be a pro athlete making a living without any kind of online presence, and that's the more traditional model of professional athletics—but the internet and your online persona is becoming more and more important. Being an influencer, on the other hand, is a career that only exists because of an online presence though it also tips into real life.

So you can look at it like this: An athlete is results/real life first, online brand second. An influencer is online brand first, results/real life second.

Athletes are going to be results-focused and more traditional in their hunt for sponsors. So a runner who's an athlete would be sending potential sponsors a race resume with past results, and how he or she does in races helps determine sponsorship dollars. Your online profile can make you more appealing to sponsors, and having a large online fan base can help you negotiate for better deals, but it's not your primary bargaining chip.

On the flip side, an influencer might just love running but not actually race seriously or at all—he or she would just be writing about it, Instagramming about musings around running, maybe making run workout videos. Your worth to a company is based on the content that you create and the image that you put out to the world. (In some ways, this can be much harder than getting on a podium!)

In many ways, an influencer will not have the same credibility as an athlete when it comes to certain types of advice, so if that's your lane, make sure you stay aware of how you're talking to your audience. An influencer won't use products in the same way as a pro athlete and may not have the same product knowledge.

Athlete's content supports the training and racing journey and also gives tips to the followers in the process. Influencer's content mapping may be different because it may only be about pretty pictures or looking good next to the bike. That's shifting more and more as athlete/influencer begins to blend, but it's just a good thing to be aware of as you're creating content.

In the current health / fitness climate, an athlete hoping to make a living obviously can help his or her career by also adding value as an influencer—very few athletes exist on race results alone anymore (and that's debatable as a good or bad thing, but it is a true thing). In most endurance sports, more teams are shutting down every year and dollars are shifting from paying for a road cycling team to paying for a couple of individual racers on, say, the gravel racing circuit. The individual racers aren't just getting wins, they're getting likes and creating content around their racing.

Is that fair to the athlete who solely focuses on his race results? Maybe, maybe not. This book isn't about the ethics of how sponsors are choosing who to work with, the point is to give you some insight into how you can better market yourself.

Freaking out about which you want to be? Good news: You can be both. And most of this advice applies to anyone in the fitness / athletic industry working as a self-employed woman (or man), whether that means you're looking for sponsors to fund a racing schedule, seeking partnerships for your nutrition-focused blog or Instagram, or hoping to create partnerships and draw more attention to your yoga studio or bring more students to your spin class.

Remember, This is a Job Hunt

In addition to simply not being a jerk, an important idea to note before we dive into some of the particulars of seeking sponsorship is this simple concept: you're trying to become an employee.

It's important to keep this in mind, regardless of your race results or how far you've come in the sport. You're still going to be asking for a job, and you're going to go through an interview process. The fastest way to turn off a sponsor is to approach the job hunt like you're doing them a favor by offering to be sponsored by them.

How can you be a good sponsored athlete? "Show up on time, come to work, be sociable... Like any good employee would," says one sponsorship coordinator who's seen hundreds of athletes come and go from sponsorships ranging from high-end luxury athlete apparel, a major footwear company, a massive bike brand, and a company that prides itself in its utilitarian-chic products.

Endurance sport—from road racing to triathlon to track running—is littered with carcasses of young racers who had all the raw talent in the world but were held back by their own arrogance. I won't name names, but virtually every sponsor interviewed in this book recalled at least one racer who got cut or didn't get hired because of their superiority complex.

And these names were ones I recognized: they were fast racers who would have won a ton... Between you and me, in the dozens of interviews I did for this book, there were three names that came up A LOT. There were also plenty of people I had never heard of. Guess why I hadn't heard of them? That's right, because they're no longer sponsored or supported because of their attitudes. Oh—and that's right, people I interviewed were more than happy to name names. People don't forget being treated badly, and most aren't afraid to tell the world about it.

"If you're looking for sponsorships, don't display arrogance, or disinter-est," added one team manager. I promise you, this will not get you onto a team, score you a sponsor, or create any lasting alliances. It will quickly get you blacklisted or at least $hit-talked the next time a bunch of industry people get together over drinks.

So what does that mean? It means you shouldn't expect people to flock to you just because you did well at one race. It means not taking a sponsor for granted once you do have one (after all, you're going to have to go through a yearly performance review at the end of the season, whether you know about it or not).

No matter how good you are, you'll do better in the industry if you stay humble, and keep acting like an ideal employee. It'll pay off in dividends (like a better job when you've retired from racing, or a move to a bigger and better team) later.

I find that the easiest way to think about this is 'if you wouldn't do/say/ act a certain way while working at a Starbucks, you probably shouldn't do it as an athlete.' What exactly does being a good 'employee' mean? I'm assuming that most of you reading this have worked in retail or the service industry before. Honestly, it's not that different.

A few tips:

Be on time (or early): Whether it's a flight you're taking to a race, or a race day autograph signing session, be ready to go when you said you would be ready to go. No excuses. When travel is involved, this becomes even more important—missed flights can mean lost contracts and jobs.

Communicate effectively: Return emails promptly, respond to voicemails from team managers or sponsors.

Understand your job description: Racing the race is often just the begin-ning. Your job might also be to post a race report after each race, per your sponsor's request. Basically, if it's in your contract or your boss has asked for it and you agreed, get it done.

Don't be a diva: Back to that 'don't be a dick' rule. It's OK to ask for what you're worth and have certain things that you need, like quiet time before a race to properly warm up, or a certain post-race routine. But if that routine gets screwed up, don't fly off the handle. Politely restate what it is you need, and assume that it will be fixed for next time.

Keep your office clean: Don't let your race-day bag spill all over the team tent.

Service with a smile: When you're showing up for work—the in-person stuff, whether it's racing, teaching, speaking, autograph signing, et cetera—try to shift into a good mood, even if you're not 100% feeling it. Your fans will appreciate the effort.

Now pause for a moment before you head to the next section, and give yourself some pats on the back and some kicks in the ass. Write down a list with a couple of examples of nice things that you did—and note if any of them led to better relationships or new connections. Then, write another column of potential screw-ups. Was there something you did that killed a potential relationship—or even just hurt one, like by being somewhat rude of a coach at a camp? If so, analyze how the new you would handle it better. If possible, send an apology. (The apology, even if it's been a while, can even help create a new, better relationship. It's amazing!)

The Importance of Standing Out

Endurance racers often aren't the most extroverted creatures… That's why most of us got into endurance sports in the first place: We race best solo. But the ones that are memorable—and the ones pulling in the biggest paychecks—are the ones who do push themselves to be extroverted (or are lucky enough to naturally be that way). Racers who have a story to tell other than "I run fast" are often easier for fans to relate to, and be interested in.

"In a gross over-simplification, it's about personality," says a longtime cycling industry veteran. "If an athlete is always on the podium but can't do the interview after and act graciously with the crowd at the event, they are of little value to the brand."

Consider two of the big names in cycling in 2018: Chris Froome and Peter Sagan. Froome obviously commands a pretty hefty paycheck, but Sagan is almost certainly making significantly more, despite similar palmares. Why? Personality—and a willingness to show it. Look up some of the crazy stuff Sagan has been up to in the last couple years: Grease musical numbers, lighting up his hometown's Christmas lights on his bike, doing a Rocky-style training montage… he's not afraid to be goofy (to the point of eating gummy bears post-race!). On the flip side, Froome gains plenty of fans, but plenty of detractors as well, because he's not the most outgoing guy in the field.

"Don't miss opportunities to share more about yourself," says one sponsorship manager at a major cycling company, highlighting this exact idea. "If someone asks you a question, answer it in-depth. Froome doesn't excite people. He's shown different sides to himself lately, and that's great, but someone like Peter Sagan is enchanting. He could take second place for the rest of his life and still be the most popular."

It's a bummer that being shy is a strike against you, but you can work around it (and you don't have to re-dub Summer Nights, Sagan-style, to do it). Think about bike races and your time on social media like being at work, and wanting to make a good impression for your boss. Your personality should be shining through via your style and your social channels.

Look at riders like Ellen Noble, who aren't merely achieving solid results. In addition to being one of the top in the world for cyclocross, the young racer did two remarkable things in the 2017 season. First, she became the first woman to bunnyhop the barriers in a cyclocross World Cup race in Iowa in the early season. Then, she parlayed that hopping—which had already brought her a ton of press and new fans—into a social statement. She started hash tagging #BunnyHopThePatriarchy to talk about women's equality issues in- and out-side of sport, and even created an Instagram to highlight rad other women in cycling as well as a t-shirt that sold well enough to raise a ton of cash for scholarships for her Quest project, a camp for teens aspiring to be pro racers someday. It's not a shock that she had her choice of programs for the 2018 season.

"If I were a young rider looking to be successful, obviously, I'd try to stand apart and stand out in the way I ride and race and carry myself," adds a sponsorship director. "I'd be really purposeful and active in building my brand. Those kids that stand out tend to have a personality, that's a force. They can readily make themselves stand apart as a person."

"I think industry support remains strong for cycling, but it's expressed in multiple manners now: events, athletes and demos. Not simply teams. Brands look for value, things like athletes that can deliver value off the race course by strong social media skills, etc." says a director for a World Cup race.

Which leads to, by the way, the fact that this edict doesn't give you permission to sit around on SnapChat all day when you should be cleaning a bike, recovering, or preparing for a race. But it does mean you want to think critically about what you're putting out into the world. (We'll talk more about the social media specifics in a later chapter.)

"We make an effort to bring people into the family and do more marketing around them. We're not just interested in the watts," adds a sponsorship coordinator. "That's tough, if your life is eight hours on the bike every day.

That's awesome and hopefully it pays off. But if you don't round out who you are as a person with other interests or can't make a conversation, you won't get far."

So, how do you stand out? The answer isn't just a good online presence. Even if you're not a top pro, you can start acting like one—preferably not one of the ones that's known as a huge jerk. Start small, with your own community, but work on finding places to host clinics and rides with you, the pro, or talks at your local bike shop. Think about what would actually be a value-add for those groups.

"I have worked with athletes that go out of their way to put on clinics and coach local clubs," says one outdoor industry veteran. "The key in that scenario is having good photographs and grabbing any media that the club or shop creates."

But with good photographs, you need to have good content in the form of videos, captions, and relatable, interesting content. In short, you have to have something to say.

One easy way? Offer to write columns for magazines and blogs, especially smaller ones. You probably won't make any extra cash doing this, but it'll set you up with a great reason why sponsors should hire you and raise your social and online cache in the process. Some of the best-paid pros never win championships. Instead, they score decent results while building a huge fan base that listens to their every word.

Take a few minutes and list the things you want to stand out for. First, list your actual athletic skill and hopes as far as your sport aspirations go. But then, think about your personality and how to make that shine through. Is it your hilarious Instagrams, or your insightful blog posts? Are you a great speaker, and think you'd be great at hosting clinics? Or are you a behind-the-scenes guy or girl who wants to really promote a certain charity?

Be Authentic, But Deliberately

Being authentic is super important, and probably the number one tip that any influencer will tell you. But while that's true, there are a few caveats to this point. You can be authentically you while keeping your audience (and your prospective audience) in mind.

My initial thought when I started writing this was to tell athletes to avoid cursing on their social media, avoid controversial posts, avoid causing a ruckus. But then, the more I thought about it, I realized that in today's world, we CAN cause a ruckus if we want to … And it might even work in your favor.

It certainly has for a former pro racer I know. She made her mark on the sport of cycling by being a self-proclaimed 'hell-raiser.' She curses on Twitter, isn't afraid to tell people to F off, and stands up for herself and all women in a way that is authentically her.

But she does so deliberately. She knows exactly what she's doing, why she's doing it, and she stays 110% true to her brand. Companies who support who know exactly what they're getting—and because of that, she gets great support from a few companies that want to support that kind of spirit.

That's what the authenticity debate tends to miss. It's great to be authentic, but you have to be mindful and tactical about how you're doing it. If you're trying to be a rep for brands that are targeted at preteens, cursing all over social probably won't get you a signed contract, nor will uber-sexy pics. But you can still post the same statements and sentiments (just sans the F bombs) and the same swimsuit pictures (just think less sexy, more fun) to get the same message across in a way that's appropriate to your audience.

A rockstar runner like Alexi Pappas is a great example of someone who stays absolutely authentic with her own voice, but also knows how to speak to her audience. Her fan base contains a lot of younger girls, so while she talks about feminist issues, gets angry, gets loud, and makes herself heard, she does it without cursing and largely keeping her rhetoric positive. She's being authentic, but she's also being deliberate by her word and photo choice.

And she could very well change it up in the future—as can you. Arguably, your authentic self should be growing and changing as you mature… and I don't just mean this to apply to teenagers, the same is true as you shift from 30 to 40.

You can always change what's authentic to you as you and your brand (and your fan base) grow, both in age and in numbers. Young athletes, as a rule, should avoid using tons of profanity. As you move into your 20s, though, you may find that you're dropping the F bomb when it makes sense and your audience—who is also now in their 20s — appreciates your candor.

A personal favorite outside-of-sport example of this is Miley Cyrus, and how she's changed what was authentic to her as she's gone from Hannah Montana to Miley-as-a-grown-woman over the years. She lost some fans in the process, but gained plenty more by being true to herself. But she wasn't trying to keep her Disney fans when she made that deliberate switch, and she knew she would see a change in her fanbase. Luckily, she was talented and famous enough that it worked for her!

One last note when it comes to authenticity: Being authentic will never/ should never excuse poor working behavior.

Seth Godin talks about this on an episode of The Tim Ferriss Show*, saying that he actually doesn't believe in being authentic. That's right, Seth freaking Godin, marketing guru of our generation, said that. He then explained that there are times when he's about to give a speech, for instance, where he doesn't feel like giving a speech. His response isn't to be authentic to that feeling and cancel, it's to go be the Seth Godin that people are paying to see and deliver the damn speech.

Yes, being authentic is great… But you also have to show up.

So if you're running into a deadline or you have a contract that you agreed to (remember, be SMART about agreeing to do anything, so I'm only saying this on the assumption that you didn't make a deal with the devil here), you have to sometimes suck it up and get it done. A company may say that they're cool with you needing some 'me' time off of social media, or say they understand that you're too stressed to deal with it right now, or forgive an email response sent five weeks too late… But they won't forget. And while they might not drop you, they may not be quite as inclined to give you a good deal ever again.

Being 'Authentic' matters. But so does being smart and thoughtful about the long-term strategies needed for your career.

*You can find that podcast at https://tim.blog/2018/11/01/seth-godin-this-is-marketing/

Think Globally, Act Locally

Unless you're already a big-name racer or influencer with hundreds of thousands of followers, a great place to start with building a following/fan base is your local scene. You can inspire closer connections, build stronger fan bases, and get local businesses on board with you and what you're trying to do—and then you can take it to a broader audience.

A lot of people in the fitness space want to start with going global—newbie yoga instructors flock to Costa Rica to showcase their teaching, bike racers want to travel to Europe to train and race. But staying at home—wherever home happens to be—can work really well for building a small but solid fan base to get you started.

Assuming that you are reading this from your current home base, whether it's at your parent's, in an apartment you're renting, or in a house that you've lived in for years, it's time to get involved in your community.

Not only will you grow your local fan base/following, you'll be setting yourself up for local sponsorships (more on that later). It's also great practice for eventually creating a worldwide fanbase.

What can you do?

Raise your 'brand awareness.' If you're racing for a certain team or trying to build your personal brand, try to wear or carry one piece of branded gear with you at all times. It may serve as a conversation starter, or even just make people start to learn the brand by osmosis.

Make a goal of having a 'regular order' at one place in town that you love. It doesn't have to be fancy or expensive! While you're patronizing your favorite spots, try to get to know the staff (not in a pushy or creepy way, just casually).

Volunteer somewhere in town, preferably doing something related to your niche. Teach a yoga class at the women's shelter, make your special healthy version of cookies for a local fundraiser, etc.

Take classes. If you're a runner looking for sponsorship dollars so you can race in Europe, taking a couple of free classes at the library in something tangentially related—like a Toastmasters public speaking session—is an easy way to meet potential fans and sponsors. If you're hoping to be a yoga teacher at a studio or start your own studio, taking classes and getting to know the local students is a smart move.

Teach classes. If you're a cyclist, why not get spin-certified and pick up some cash working at the local YMCA or spin studio while telling your students about your goals for the season? If you're a triathlete who's really into sports nutrition, can you pitch a class at the local continuing-ed school on healthy cooking? If you're not sure about your teaching skills, maybe consider trying to find an assistant / intern-type teaching or coaching position—most high school sports teams are happy for any assistance. (Teaching isn't for everyone, but it is a really fast way to get entrenched in the community.)

Get in with local media. Local town/county newspapers and magazines are constantly looking for content. You may not get paid to write for a local paper or to do an interview for a local website, but it's great local exposure, a resume builder, and practice for when you're asked to do an interview for a bigger publication.

One caveat: Don't go so hyper-local that you can't branch out, though: Don't change the name of your website or social media channels to TOWN + YOUR NAME, or only post only local content. You still want the broad range appeal for growing your base of support outside of town as well.

People Smell Bull$hit

Bad news, boys and girls: people are pretty good at smelling bull$hit and weeding out phonies. So all that stuff about being nice I said in the first chapter, well, you have to actually mean it.

"At some point, you can't make shit up," says Jeremy Powers, four-time National Champion and arguably America's most popular pro cyclocrosser. The thing is, no one else can be Jeremy Powers. The guy is a legend for a good reason: his extroverted personality shines, he's passionate about the sport, he's genuinely that fun, goofy, loud guy you saw at races and on Behind THE Barriers. When he retired, he immediately got recruited to continue acting as a TV host for another cycling media channel.

And I've seen a lot of people try to be him. We did a lot of work together in the last eight years of his career, and in that time, I've seen a ton of younger racers try to emulate him. Some even started Behind THE Barriers-styled projects. I've never seen one of them succeed, because at the end of the day, no one wants Jeremy Powers 2.0, they're happy with Jeremy, the original. Not to mention, any 2.0 version of him tends to come off as flaky, inauthentic, and not nearly as awesome as the original.

While I talk a lot in here about how to give a good interview and be a good representation to your sponsors, it bears mentioning that while there are certain principles of etiquette that exist, you also need to lead with authenticity. Try to be someone you're not, and it'll get flagged instantly.

If you're not a perky cheerleader stereotype from a nineties chick flick, don't act like one. (If you are, good for you. Own that $hit.)

You've probably seen the cheesy memes on Instagram already: Be You. Be Your Authentic Self. Authenticity is Everything. It's mostly true. Like I said earlier, if your authentic self swears like a sailor and rarely spell checks, you may want to tone that down. But if your authentic self is a Harry Potter-loving nerd who happens to race cross-country crazy-fast, own that. (Harry Potter socks definitely are a great accessory choice.)

People will respond to you being yourself, and they'll know pretty quickly if you're trying to put on a facade. Figure out what makes you the most 'you,' and own it.

For me, the best way to work on defining yourself and how you want to be seen is by thinking about how you'd want a celebrity profile of you to read. Sounds silly, but it really helps hone in on what makes you unique and what you want to be known for. While there are plenty of great examples within the sporting community, I love looking beyond that and looking at all different types of profiles to get a better sense of what it means to be authentically you, and described as such.

I love this one from Outside Magazine: "While Erika Bergman jokes that her petite size launched her career, her mechanical and scientific knowledge are what led her to the waters in the Caribbean, Arctic, and West Coast—and into classrooms across the world as a champion for female engineers. Bergman's life reads something like a young adult adventure novel. At just 15 years old, she talked her way into a gig as the diesel engineer aboard a tall ship that was traveling from California to Canada."

Or this one, also in Outside Magazine and a bit more to the point: "Jessie Graf is a badass."

Great anecdotes, great introductions. That's how you want to be written about. (Now, imagine the intro you get if you're trying to be someone you're not.)

Take a stab at writing your own celebrity profile. If that's too intense, think about it this way: What are 5 adjectives you'd like people to ascribe to you? What's a one-sentence description of yourself that you'd love someone to write? Once you have an idea of ways you'd like to be described, just keep them in mind when talking to people at races, posting on social media, updating your blog, etc. For example, if you want to be known as optimistic and cheerful, social media posts complaining about what went wrong in a race aren't going to be very helpful.

To end this chapter on an emphatic note, here's a profile of me that was written in 2017 that serves as one of my all-time high points in my life:

How does a bookworm, who admittedly couldn't run a mile until she was 20, wind up completing her second Ironman, serving as the team manager for a U.S. cyclocross team, writing a book series encouraging female cyclists, all while carving out a home in Collingwood? If this sounds like an unimaginable transformation (and a crazy schedule), you haven't met Molly Hurford yet. Small in stature, Molly is mighty in all other respects. She's passionate about cycling, about women in sport and about her adopted Canadian community. We caught up with Molly shortly after she finished her second Ironman.

excerpt from Mountain Life Magazine, words by Alison Kennedy

Self-Promote in Unexpected Ways

13

You can Instagram or Tweet about sponsors until your fingers are numb while training for 30 hours a week, but another great and arguably equally important way to get noticed is to self-promote in ways that don't involve social media, or, at least, don't center around social media. Here are a few ways, but feel free to think outside the box!

Help Out with Charity Event
Not only do you get to put in some miles, you can be helpful and charitable at the same time. Potential sponsors love seeing riders who are already giving back to the community and have a few charities that they support. It makes you more well-rounded, and just generally a better person (and, on a more mercenary note, a better proposition as an athlete). And while you're there, don't just keep your head down and do the ride or run, chat with people as you go—you're not here to race!

Host Nights at Your Local Shop
Whether it's an autograph signing or Q&A at a local shop that sponsors you, or just a meet and greet at a shop in a town that's hosting a race, this is a great way to turn interested spectators and acquaintances into actual fans of you and your racing. That's the conversion we want—real life likes and kudos. Not to mention, this is a great way to fake it til you make it: Create a buzz around yourself until it actually becomes a reality. You may need to offer to organize the event yourself—don't expect a shop to do all of the work for you.

Volunteer Your Time at Races
Ask promoters how you can help them: Is there a kiddie clinic the day before your race that you could help with? Could you spend a day doing course markings? Things like that go a long way to ensuring that you

always get free registration plus hook-ups with things like host housing. Organizers also often deal with the sponsorship coordinators for different companies, and can give them positive feedback about you.

Show Up to a Mid-Week Series and Help Out
Promoters often run local mid-week series and these can be a great chance to get in a workout (even if you know you'll be the fastest one there). They also present a good chance to chat with people, help out new riders and generally make a good name for yourself. Offer to help out if you want to get bonus points, and always stick around to chat at the end—like a charity event, just showing up won't get you very far. Use this time to form connections.

Commit.
If you say you're going to do something, do it. All of these things will take time away from work and training, so make sure that you're not overcommitting. In almost every case, bailing on something you've committed to is much worse than if you had never signed up for it at all.

Are you noticing a trend in that all of these are fairly low-key small-town events? It doesn't need to be a huge signing that brings in thousands of fans to make sponsors happy. That one-on-one time you can have with people at events like these develops true fans who will follow your career for years to come.

Think of a few different events/ways you can self-promote this season. (And then, actually start sending some emails/laying the groundwork for one of them. But don't try all of these activities at once, plan one thing at a time so you don't end up overwhelmed and dropping the ball.)

THINKING ABOUT SPONSORSHIPS

CHART 2

What Can You Offer Sponsors?

Ask not what your sponsors can do for you, but what you can do for your sponsors.

Of course we want a sponsor that will help us. That's obvious. And you definitely shouldn't seek out sponsors who have gear or services that you don't want. But when approaching sponsors and negotiations, it's smart to think about the sponsor's side of the equation, not your own.

One longtime pro put it perfectly: View yourself as an extension of the brand's marketing division.

The first thing a sponsor want to know is how you can help them, not vice versa. Occasionally, there are sponsors who just love the sport, but even those fans want to see some kind of return on investment, which could simply mean having a friendly face at the race. But offering a sponsor a small piece of space on a jersey or singlet is no longer is enough for most brands.

In fact, when you're already on a racing team—one that might be great, but isn't giving you a lot of cash money, or is missing a critical product (like sports nutrition), you might want to go after individual sponsors, but a space on your kit for a logo is completely out of the question. Now, you have nothing to offer… Or do you?

Really, the space on a kit is only so useful to a sponsor. Sure, it's nice to see the logo out there, but how many close-up photos of the back of your jersey are making it into cycling publications? How many people are buying a certain ride food because a 20-year-old who doesn't win every race is wearing the logo? Most people aren't going to see you eat that ride food anyway, so how will they know you're into it? The old model of "iron a logo onto your shirt and call it a day" is gone—now, athletes need to think outside the box.

As you collect data to approach sponsors, think about all the ways you might be able to work for them:

Your social media reach
Across all of your feeds, how many people follow you? How many likes does an average post get? (This isn't a 'buy followers' suggestion, and the number itself should be honest, not a faux-inflated number. We'll talk more about social media later.)

Your website
Do you get traffic to your website? Is it updated and current? (Do you even have one? More on that later as well.)

Events and races
What races are you attending, and are there any charity events or fun rides on your schedule? Are you hosting group rides or local events? (If not, can you host a group ride?)

Non-racing clothing
Can you still wear another brand's t-shirt or hat at races? What can you do to show off what the sponsor is giving you?

Swag handouts
Can you hand out samples at races or host giveaways?

Media
Are you a regular on any websites, podcasts, Facebook Lives, etc. for companies/magazine/websites already?

Take a few minutes and brainstorm a list of creative ways that you can help promote potential sponsors outside of riding your bike or running quickly. Don't forget, the faster you go, the more blurred that logo gets! (This list will come in handy when you're negotiating or writing a cover letter to a new potential sponsor.)

Spend Money to Make Money (AKA Test Before You Ask)

We'll get into approaching sponsors for gear and goodies in a bit, but first thing's first: know what you like and what you need in order to be the most effective athlete you can be. When you work with a sponsor or partner, you need to believe in their product. If you endorse everything or every trend that you're asked to or paid to, your followers and fans are going to sense that you're not being real with them, and you'll lose a ton of credibility. There's nothing more annoying than an athlete who's promoting cricket protein one week, a ketone supplement the next and a whacky new recovery tool two days later. It starts to seem really inauthentic, really fast. And even the more 'normal' stuff, like a bike, goggles or running shoes can be tricky if you're willing to use literally anything that's handed to you.

It's important to know what you like, and what works for you. I know you won't be able to buy a ton of bikes (or other pricey gear) to test, but you can go to test ride events or borrow friend's bikes for rides. You can buy single serve packets of lots of foods and drink mixes to try, and you can at least try on clothing and shoes in stores.

There are a couple of reasons for this: First, because it helps you be authentic in seeking partnerships. If you only seek sponsorships from brands that you actually like and currently use, you're not going to end up in a situation where you're being asked to endorse something you hate.

The general rule of thumb is: Don't endorse what you wouldn't buy with your own hard-earned money. It's disingenuous, and it's a crappy thing to do to your fans who might actually be spending their hard-earned money on this thing that you're promoting. The brand itself will also likely pick up on the fact that you don't love the product. Ever watch a video or listen to a podcast with an advertisement that makes you think, 'I bet that person doesn't even use XYZ?' You can usually tell when someone genuinely likes the thing they're promoting.

The other reason it pays to buy and test products before you approach a brand? It saves you from ending up with a bunch of crappy products that you now have to use. If you're a runner and you know you only like 8mm drop trail-specific sneakers, is it worth approaching a shoe brand or a local running shop that doesn't have the one thing that you want? A sponsorship doesn't mean much if it puts you in gear that doesn't make you perform at your best.

The other reason to know what you like is that when you're finally talking to sponsors, you know what you want so you won't end up getting their throwaway stuff. Honestly? A lot of brands that are willing to sponsor a lot of athletes will often give the newer, 'lower-tier' athletes and influencers last year's product, factory seconds, and the flavors or types of gear that didn't sell well. Then, you're stuck with crap that no one wanted to buy.

But if you go in knowing that you like XY flavor or product? That's doing your homework and showing brand loyalty before you're paid to be loyal. It's impressive to see people—especially younger riders—who've done their homework, and are willing to support brands before the brands support them. They'll understand that you're serious about wanting them as sponsors, not just asking every brand for the same generic things.

I see so many racers end up with sponsors that have gear/food/clothing that they don't actually want or need, but they're so excited at the idea of 'getting sponsored' that they take what they can get… And live to regret it.

Start figuring out your wish list now. Give yourself a reasonable budget—could be $20, could be $2000—and think about what you can try out with that. Then, start trying. Keep notes somewhere on each product, so you can refer back and speak about each with the expertise of someone who's been there, done that. Potential sponsors will love you for your willingness to offer feedback, and you won't end up with three boxes of gels that give you diarrhea.

For example:
Brand X Gels—tested 5/1 in road race. Felt really fast and didn't have digestive problems.
Brand Y Gels—tested 5/10 in time trial. Instantly felt bloated and the sweet taste was gross.

Don't have the cash to try everything? You can still check out local (and non-local) shops to try on shoes, clothing, helmets, etc. without buying (try to be as polite as possible and buy something, even if it's just a tube or CO2 cartridge if you're doing this). There are also often shop-sponsored Demo Days where you can test new bikes and gear, which are great no-cost options.

It's easy to get sucked in by short term gains: not needing to buy new running shorts or ride food or a bike for the season sounds great, but if the shoe doesn't fit, then you're likely going to suffer during the season and end up unhappy in the long run. And you run the serious risk of missing out on finding the sponsors that are the best fit (literally and figuratively) for you.

Lastly—the other reason that testing before you reach out is a great idea is because in addition to finding stuff you love, you can actually do some posts (yes, posting about stuff that you bought, without getting paid to post about it) on your social media. Tell people about the brand and your favorite stuff before you reach out to the brand. Then, when you do reach out, you might have already gotten on their radar because they saw you tagging that pair of running shorts on social media and saw that it got a lot of likes and comments. It's a simple way to add value before asking for anything, which puts you in a much stronger position with a potential sponsor.

How Do You Choose Sponsors To Go After?

This is obviously the entire point of this book: getting sponsors, and keeping them. After all, most races don't exactly pay out the big bucks, even to the winners. So sponsorship dollars are… well, they're solid gold. While some sponsors may come to you, this is a 'broad strokes' look at what normally goes into getting a new sponsor. And it starts with what and who you already know.

Don't worry: we'll get into approaching them in a later chapter, but for now, just start by figuring out who you want to work with. But this is actually where I see most athletes making a big mistake: They either wait for sponsors to approach them and never really think about what it is that they're looking for, or they use a shotgun-style approach of sending out tons of generic sponsorship proposals to dozens of similar companies hoping that something sticks. But the athletes who get great sponsorship deals and start long-term relationships are the ones who approach sponsors more strategically.

Make a List
Who are the brands you'd love to work with? Think back to what we just talked about: Who's stuff do you actually use and love? Big, small, local, global, it doesn't matter. Just start with a list of brands that you admire, that you already like and would happily use. Sure, there are cash sponsorships from companies you don't necessarily utilize, but for starters, think about what you'd want to be repping, in a perfect world.

Refine the List
Make sure that your list includes some realistic options. We can't all get Nike and Monster Energy, but most of us can find a local yoga studio that would give us some free class passes. Think about local businesses that you already support, like your favorite local bakeshop or microbrewery.

Note Your WHY for Each

Next to each sponsor you've listed, write a quick sentence about why you want that company behind you. Try to think of both physical and culture-based reasons. For a bike brand like Trek, you might say, "I love their Fuel EX mountain bikes, and I like that they're really committed to women's racing and growing the sport." This serves a few purposes. It'll help when it comes time to make the pitch, because you're thinking specifically about the brand and what they stand for. It also helps you decide what it is that you want to ask for from the sponsor, so you're getting specific about what gear you love. And lastly, it might help you cross a few brands off the list. You may have listed an energy drink company because you know it would be super prestigious to be sponsored by them, but you may not actually like the drink! Maybe it's a good idea to cross that one off (for now, at least).

Look for Connections

Go through each brand you've listed, and note if you have any connections (a friend racing for a team sponsored by the company already, a cousin who works in the local bike shop you always go to). Once you've done that, then look at the brands that didn't have a connection, and try to scale down in order to find one. If, for example, you listed Smith Optics on there but don't know anyone at the company, do you perhaps know someone at the local bike shop that carries Smith? (You don't need to know someone to approach a company, but that initial connection certainly helps, especially early in your career!)

Gently Reach Out

This is where most people fall short. Reaching out doesn't mean sending a text to a buddy that just asks for help, or emailing a form email and race resume to someone you know at a company. We're going to hand-tailor your ask: who are you, why are you asking, what makes the product one that you want to rep, et cetera. If it's a local business, hand-deliver your request rather than emailing it. Don't worry: We'll get into this more later, in a lot more depth—but for now, maybe consider deepening that connection. Head into the local bike shop to chat with employees, make plans to ride with the cyclist you know who's sponsored by the brand you love, et cetera.

Informal Interviews

When it comes to choosing what sponsors or teams you want to work with, rather than looking at the swag that the team has, start by looking at the athletes who are already working with the sponsor/team.

Most pro athletes, especially in endurance sport, are easier to approach and chat with than you might expect. They're happy to answer questions that are thoughtfully asked, whether you try to speak to them in real life at an event or message them on social media.

Start with your more local scene: Are there any athletes living near you who you admire? Try to reach out and see if you can meet for a run, a ride, coffee, whatever. This informal hangout can give you a great chance to speak to them about how they found their way onto their current team and what their best tips are, and sometimes (not always) can net you a recommendation from that athlete when you do apply for their team. They also may know of smaller or similar teams who are actively looking for new racers.

Spending time with an athlete who's already 'made it' is great early in your career for a few reasons. It can show you one person's pathway to success, it can show you the mistakes that you can avoid, it can help you develop a new friendship, and it can offer you a more realistic vision of what your future as a pro athlete might hold.

Honestly, that last point is arguably the most important. I've mentioned it a couple times already, but the life of an endurance athlete is a lot harder than it looks, and it's important to understand that as you start to commit to this as your lifestyle and career plan. It's not for everyone, and spending time with a pro racer may serve to show you that you're happy racing seriously… But maybe not as your actual career.

You'll be amazed at how kind and down-to-earth most pro athletes are, and even that can be a huge benefit to you: It's a great reminder than in addition to being fast and good at your sport, you need to be a good person as well if you're going to find success.

It's amazing how much knowledge many of these pro athletes have—both in terms of racing tactics and training tips but also in terms of how to talk to certain sponsors or team managers, how to schedule social media and balance it with training, and so much more.

So don't be shy about reaching out to pro athletes to try to set up these informal 'interviews.' You might even end up with a new training buddy in the process!

(Of course, not every pro athlete is going to be willing to make this kind of time for you, so don't be offended if your request is met with radio silence. Don't be pushy: Some athletes are surprisingly shy and introverted, or they have lives that you don't see on social media and are busy. Move on if you don't hear back.)

Market Yourself as YOU

Now that you have your dream list of partners, look at what makes them similar. You might start to notice trends—and you might notice that certain brands fit together really well, while others don't have much in common. What you're trying to do is create a master list of beloved brands that represent you, and brands that you feel embody your personal style.

"If you absolutely love a certain brand, it likely has characteristics and a style that separates it from similar ones," says one sponsorship coordinator. "Find the partners and sponsors that are as natural as they can be to you, and shift your lexicon to that."

What he means here is that someone who's looking for a Rapha sponsorship will present him or herself in a different way than someone looking to impress Monster energy drinks, for example. The vibes are different. Think about your personal style—this isn't just a 'girl thing,' by the way: guys have just as much of a unique vibe—and think about what brands best fit your particular personality, how you dress, how you race, how you present yourself on social media.

If your favorite brands seem super out-of-place with your current vibe, can you pivot slightly to be more in line with their style? This doesn't—and shouldn't—mean a whole new wardrobe or attitude, just some tweaks. For example, if you're aiming for a brand that focuses heavily on children's gear or you're looking for a sponsorship from a 'family-friendly' local bike shop, you probably want to avoid cursing on your social media channels and could maybe consider helping out at a local kid's ride.

"The best people in the world are chameleons who know when it's time to dot their i's and cross their t's and be really buttoned up, and when it's time to be a little more casual with a brand," adds one sponsorship manager. "You have to be f***ing smart. You have to look for opportunities, you have to read the room. Don't come into a more high-end boutique brand suggesting that you're going to light yourself on fire and jump trash cans. If you come to a brand with a different vibe, though, maybe that's the approach you could take."

Of course, some brands don't have specific styles: A company like Nike is so large that it appeals to all different demographics, so regardless of your personal style, you could likely fit in. However, you can still think more critically about your best marketing strategies by looking at some of the athletes that are currently sponsored by Nike and seeing what makes them stand out in the crowd.

Take a few minutes and make a list of adjectives that describe your personal style. ("Edgy," "Fearless," "Colorful," for example. Then, look at your list of ideal sponsors. Who on that list would share most of those adjectives? More bluntly put, what sponsors' social media feeds come closest to resembling yours? That's a great sign of a good fit, especially if you haven't been looking at their page and trying to emulate it on purpose.

If you're having trouble seeing those connections and realizing that you don't really have a specific "marketing plan" (for lack of a better term), think about how you can make your personality shine through more clearly. What can you shift slightly to better align with your dream sponsors? Think tiny shifts, not major lifestyle overhauls: You are your greatest selling point, and if you try to change too drastically, you're likely not going to be able to keep up that public persona.

Don't Forget the "Little Guy"

Often, athletes seek out sponsorships from the obvious choices: companies in the bike industry that manufacture bikes, helmets, kit, accessories, sunglasses... But what often gets neglected is the roll of smaller, local businesses, which often have more willingness to help out new-to-the-sport athletes. This comes back to 'think global, act local.'

Consider approaching your local run shop, brewery where local rides end, yoga studio, or massage therapist as well as the standard industry companies and major teams, especially if you're trying to put together a solo program and not just gain entry onto a team. These small sponsorships add up—even if it's just discounts at the run shop and a free monthly massage. Often, because those places don't sponsor multiple athletes or deal in massive budgets, they're excited to help promote you and be promoted by you.

Additionally, garnering good relationships with smaller local business can ultimately help you with those bigger-ticket sponsorships. If you have a resume and references list that's full of people who are happy with the return on investment they've had with you, a big company will look more favorably at you. It also shows that you're willing to put in work with sponsors, not just chase long-shots.

And a word of wisdom on the local bike, run or triathlon shop? Don't forget, if your local bike shop, for example, sells Trek Bicycles and you're racing well for them and doing a lot of events with them, the owner is likely going to mention you to the distributor, or to the higher-ups in the company. The cycling industry, like the running and triathlon industries, is a small, close-knit group of passionate people. That little store that hooked you up could lead to a major deal with one of the brands that they carry, so keep that in mind when you're feeling down about going with small sponsors versus chasing the big ones.

These smaller sponsorships may not seem as sexy as, say, a Red Bull or Oakley sponsorship. But until you really hit the big time, the bigger companies either won't come near you, or if you do get in with them, you're likely going to be more a cog in the machine versus someone that they actually promote. On the flip side, that local bike shop is going to be hosting rides with you, putting your poster up, and singing your praises (if you play your cards right). The little guys out there are the ones who care—who really are passionate about you and the sport.

When trying to approach local companies, think about businesses outside of your industry. A spin class teacher/influencer can work with a local cafe to help them promote a new healthy menu, a runner can score a sponsorship with a local masseuse in exchange for some social media love.

As you make a list of companies to approach, think about the places that you already frequent as starting points. You don't want to end up sponsored by a cafe that makes the worst coffee in town, or a bike shop that rarely gets work done on time. You want to work with businesses that you truly like and believe in: If you wouldn't patronize them now, don't ask them for money or sponsorships.

When approaching a shop owner for the first time, have a plan in mind: A lot of store owners will be generally interested, but you'll have better results if you already have a list of a few ways you and the shop can work together. What can you do for them, and what do you want from them? Starting with a concrete pitch is much better than a wishy-washy 'I'd love to work together.' So many athletes I've seen have come to brands or shops and gotten a positive reception when they wanted to 'do something together,' but because they didn't have a specific list of things that they wanted from the shop, or ways to work together, the enthusiasm quickly died off. You can be open to suggestion, but having a starting point sets up the idea of what you're hoping for.

As you're starting out, don't expect a lot of businesses to be interested in coming on board with $$$$, especially if you have a small following / aren't well-known in town. Understand that you'll likely be starting out with a trade of product-for-promotion, and that maybe next season, if it goes well, you can start adding cash to the negotiations. Some shops may surprise you and have a budget, but in general, don't expect to walk away with much money.

Lastly, remember that just because it's a local business or family-run company versus a major corporation doesn't mean you should give this sponsor any less attention. Keep those sponsors happy and treat them the same as you would a huge company.

Get started: List a few local businesses that you have ties with (or maybe even places that have reached out to you in the past). Next day you have free, go into those businesses... But don't go in to drop off a resume yet. Start by just saying hi and making your presence known—no shop owner wants to support someone who they've never even met.

Remember You Can *Buy* Sunglasses

Especially as a younger and new athlete to the sport, any sponsorship at all can seem incredible. Free swag? Hells yeah! Especially when it comes from a bigger brand that's really cool to be associated with.

But here's the thing: You need to look at the value of all of your teams, funding and sponsors and remember who's actually putting money into you, versus who's newest or who seems the coolest at the time.

For example, say you ride for a local shop team. You get two bikes every season, plus some kit, and the shop's mechanics work on your bike all season and even come to a few races to support you. That's a fantastic deal, but it's not quite as cool as saying you're sponsored by a major brand.

That local shop may not seem as baller as, say, a sunglasses sponsorship from a major worldwide brand, but if that sponsorship is just a pair of glasses, it's not nearly as important to your bottom line.

But for a lot of young racers I see, the biggest brand = the one that they talk up the most and the one that they're most excited by. Unfortunately, spending all of your social media waxing poetic about your sick shades isn't a great idea. That "little local shop" that's been supporting you for years might decide to drop you from the roster next season—and for good reason—leaving you with... a pair of sunglasses.

Talking to some of the bigger companies that do solo sponsorships for riders already on teams, the sponsors all noted that a rider's 'commitment to current team' is actually a plus, and they aren't impressed with a rider that forgets about their primary sponsors in favor of chasing smaller solo deals. That doesn't make them want to give you a bigger deal, it just warns them that you don't have a great attention span and you're likely going to forget about them when something new and shiny comes along.

It's easy math:

SHOP SPONSORSHIP	SUNGLASSES SPONSORSHIP
Bikes: $7,000	Sunglasses, 2 pairs: $250
Kit: $800	
Mechanic work (over season): $1,500	
Various 'stuff' (tubes, tires, CO2s): $800	
Total: $9,100	Total: $250

So, looking at that, who seems worth impressing?

And remember—you can always buy those sunglasses at cost. Is it worth losing your primary sponsor? Likely, not.

Try making a spreadsheet similar to the one above, listing the names of each sponsor or team that you're on, what they give you (and a rough monetary value associated with it—look up the full prices of your gear online). Also make a row for notes on what each sponsor is asking of you. Are any of the expectations not in line with how much you're getting? Are you fulfilling all of the promises you've made?

QUALITY, Not Quantity, When Pitching

Picture this: you're a team manager/mechanic and you're hanging out at your team tent on a race morning. A junior cyclist walks up to you and introduces himself. He pitches you: the XY team is his favorite, has been since he was a kid and he's always dreamed of riding for you. He leaves a race resume, says thank you for any consideration, and walks away.

Seems like a pretty solid intro, right? If you're that manager, you're probably taking a few minutes to read the resume and consider interviewing the rider.

Until… Literally 10 feet away at the next tent over, you spot the same racer, chatting up the other team manager. And saying THE EXACT SAME THING.

Sounds ridiculous, reading it, right? I've seen it happen multiple times.

Two things will happen here, both with the same ending:

Manager #1 will see the rider go to the next guy and assume/overhear that the rider is making the exact same pitch.

Or… Team managers are generally quite friendly with each other—in endurance sports, team managers and mechanics spend a lot of time together at races—and will chat later, and both managers will realize that the racer has fed them the same lines.

It's one thing to approach multiple teams—that's just smart if you're hoping to find a squad. However, the dumb mistake too many riders make is making their shopping around obvious and their pitches disingenuous.

The same thing is true about emailing pitches out to different companies: If you don't take time to personalize them and really speak to the brand that you're approaching, you're unlikely to have your email be read or responded to.

If you're not going to spend time making a quality pitch for that company, why the hell would they want to devote time, resources and money into you?

As with your training, and I'm sure your coach has told you a million times, it's about QUALITY, not quantity. Sending one pitch or giving one pitch in person per week is a pretty good way to keep a steady flow of proposals and applications rolling and avoid making social gaffs or internet gaffs (i.e forgetting to take out the line about loving Nike when pitching to Adidas).

People going from tent to tent making the same pitch is a huge pet peeve for the owner of one of the biggest pro teams in mountain biking right now… And he's never hired one of the racers who did that. As a former team manager, I've gotten a lot of applications from young riders, and on more than one occasion, I've deleted the email. Not because the rider wasn't a great cyclist with stellar results, but because he accidentally didn't change the name of the team he's applying to in his clearly-formulaic email that he was sending around to every team.

Nothing makes a team manager feel less special than knowing someone is sending the same exact request to each and every team. It makes us feel lied to and like the racer doesn't care where he ends up as long as someone is paying the bills.

While that might be true for you, you should at least pretend to care about the culture of the team and what other intangibles they can provide, like great mentorship opportunities, advice, et cetera. And later in your career, you'll start to realize just how important team culture really is for your happiness, well-being and longevity in the sport you're in.

Have one great pitch per race versus 10 shitty ones. Focus on that one team, politely chatting with the manager, complimenting the riders on their recent races, and showcasing your own talent and poise. And hey, if that team doesn't work out, you can always approach another team—just don't do it at the same time, at the same race, when the tents are next to each other. Space it out.

For emails to teams, send one every few days and make sure that you get specific about what it is that you love about the team. Try to find those intangibles: Things like "I love how after every race, you're all always hanging out in the team tent laughing together. I want to be on a team that genuinely enjoys spending time together." That kind of observation stands out to the team manager who's reading your email, and thinking like that may also help you decide on which teams you actually do want to be a part of—not just which teams will take you.

I guarantee you'll have better results and more interviews if you do it that way.

So, get started! Make a list of the teams / sponsors you'd like to approach this year, maybe a few notes around those team cultures and the 'why you want them', and then make a timeline so you don't end up trying to cram in a bunch of conversations in the course of a single weekend. Spread it out during your season, and you'll be much more likely to have success in your discussions, and cultivate much better relationships.

Approaching Solo Sponsorships While on a Team

This might sound super specific, but plenty of us are on teams—your club cross-country team, for example, might not feel like a super serious thing, but they could very easily get annoyed if you're shopping around for shoe sponsors when they get a deal through New Balance already.

Team applications versus a solo sponsorship request vary slightly. And if you're already on a team, the solo sponsorships become a little more gray-area and difficult to navigate. On one hand, more money/stuff for you is a good thing. On the other, what will your team say if you're making these moves and not thinking about the good of the team?

If you're already on a team, make sure you're cleared to approach brands for solo sponsorship. Even if it's a casual team that you're on or a club that you're a part of, you will piss people off if you haven't had this conversation before starting your search.

Often it's not an issue, and problem solved. But sometimes, a team will have a few rules around personal sponsorship stuff. For example, if you're sponsored by a bike shop and a wheel company wants to give you a wheel sponsorship, but those wheels aren't sold at the shop... The shop might have a problem with that. That's fair, for two reasons: 1) If customers can't get the product you're using from your primary sponsor, how are you helping the shop? and 2) Does the shop know how to / want to work with those wheels and repair and maintain them as needed?

This is a tricky one: you have to weigh individual sponsors super carefully. It's great to have those relationships—obviously, big ones like Red Bull are a dream come true—but if you're not careful, you can quickly end up bogged down with a ton of highly-individualized requests and stuck with gear that pisses your team managers and mechanics off.

You also could end up with such a huge list of small-scale sponsors that your team is just plain irritated because every post you do is about one of the smaller sponsors, and you're so focused on juggling those sponsorships that you completely forget about being a good team player.

Once you've clarified what you're allowed to do, when approaching individual sponsors make sure you think about the angles and think about how you'll be able to work with them (or things that you won't be able to do for them because of your current team).

With solo sponsorship, the "what can I do for you?" question becomes even less about just results and race wins, and more about other factors, like having a column in a magazine, a large social media following, or events that you regularly host. That's because the brand is looking directly at you as a person as well as an athlete, not the team as a whole. It can be hard to balance these things, but make sure that your performance for the team (and for yourself) doesn't slip as a result.

It sounds tough, but solo sponsorships really are great because when a team changes hands, kicks you off (sorry!), you age off of it, or the team just dissolves (which happens all-too-often in the endurance world), it's really nice to have sponsors that will stick with you so you're not back at square one. So even if you are on a great team, it's never a bad idea to seek out individual sponsors—it just means you need to be more careful about how you do it and what you ask for.

This is also a great use of super-local sponsors, like a massage therapist or local health food store, if you're on a team that isn't local to the area. With more business-based and less industry-based sponsors, you're less likely to step on any toes or ruffle any feathers.

So, if you're on a team, think about it: Are there any easy solo sponsorships you can go after? Before you send those intro emails, make sure you know what you're allowed to offer them—and that it's OK with your team. Remember, since they likely won't get space on your pre-printed jersey / team gear, you need to have a list of more that you can offer to them.

What Should You Ask Sponsors For?

It's tempting to go straight for the big stuff: five bikes, ten pairs of wheels, a boatload of cash. But if you're just starting out in the pro side of the sport, step back and think critically and know what you actually need versus what you want.

First, assess what you really need to make it through a season. Write out your race calendar, with all the relevant info on each race: date, place, nearby airport, if you need a car rental or housing, and a bit about the race itself. Note some race specifics too, like how prestigious is it, have you done well there in the past, what's the field size like, et cetera. (Details like that might help convince sponsors that helping get you to that particular race is worth more than a local grassroots race.)

Next, write out a rough budget, thinking about airfare, race entry, bike maintenance, food, housing, car rentals, paying a mechanic (if you're racing mountain bikes or cyclocross), and general maintenance of you (sports massage, supplements, nutrition). Then, list out what gear you're going to need for the season, from head to toe.

Once you have that—make it as bare bones as you can for right now—you have an idea of how much the season is going to cost you, which helps give you an idea of what to ask for… Or at least, what your starting point is. You may not get everything that you want or need, but it's important to know what the season is going to require.

When it comes to gear, make your VERY SPECIFIC wishlist well ahead of messaging sponsors, so you aren't caught out when they offer to send you "what you need," and you then have to quickly decide what you want and rush the process. For bigger ticket items, like a full bike, have a few models that you'd be happy with decided on, and be familiar with the specs, the geometry, and enough details that if you're asked for your preferred stem length, or the marketing manager wants to talk to you about why you love the specific model, you're not completely tongue-tied. (Sponsors can smell BS from a mile away, so having a real reason you love this year's geometry is a smart move.)

And think long term, not just racing needs: What will you need to get through a season? Do you need more than one type of bike? "Boy, is this one misunderstood!" says one former sponsorship director for a major bike brand. "Gear goes without saying if a brand is sponsoring you. If a brand sponsors an athlete for mountain biking, the last thing the brand needs is the athlete doing her road training on another brand's bike. Now, in cycling, that may mean that the road bike is on loan for the season and comes back, whereas the MTB is the rider's to keep. This is all in the contract, or should be. The bikes that remain the property of the rider should be considered part of the financial remuneration." We'll talk about negotiation later, but remember this: Gear isn't necessarily 'yours,' unless you make sure that it's written into your contract. You might be required to return it at the end of the season otherwise.

While it's not a bad idea to take what you can get from a sponsor, it's not wise to get excited about a $300 full-season sponsorship when each race weekend is costing $1500 in expenses. It's easy to accidentally end up overcommitting to a sponsor who isn't giving you enough cash to fund the races that they now expect you to be at.

(See the chapter on buying the damn sunglasses for more on this.)

When you are making your pitch to a potential sponsor, it's helpful to be specific when asking for product, or letting a company know that you're asking for money. Otherwise, you might end up with a great, super positive response… that nets you a bunch of stuff that you didn't really need. Pro tip: Food and hydration sponsorships are awesome, but honestly, you don't really need that much sports drink or gel throughout a season, and those gels won't help cover gas for travel or a hotel room.

So write out a rough budget and budget proposal for your season, taking into account gear, travel, race registration and lodging. Also add in a projected cost of living expenses: food, basic necessities. You may not have enough cache to get a sponsor to pony up enough cash to live on for the season, but as an exercise, it's important to know what the next few months are going to cost overall, so you can plan accordingly—and so you're not thrilled when a sponsor offers you $100 per week, if your cost of living is $400.

In this game, knowledge is power. Even as a junior living at home with your parents, try to come up with a rough idea of how much your food, cell phone, toiletries, et cetera, add up to—you might not be paying for those things just yet, but you will be soon enough.

This can also help you plan how much you need to work in the offseason to fund your racing if you don't score enough cash sponsors.

Just a reminder: You may not get everything that you listed on that original wish list. That's okay. But knowing what you want will put you much closer to actually getting it. Don't leave these decisions entirely in the hands of sponsors. Take charge of your own career.

What to Do When They Come to You

I see a lot of juniors and young riders (and hey, I'll be honest, a lot of masters and pro riders!) get really excited when sponsors approach them. Especially at the start of your career, it can be really tempting to say YES to everything. But before you say yes to any type of team/sponsor, there are a few questions worth asking.

Ask yourself:
-What is the product? Is it well-reviewed, is the company real?
-Why are they approaching me?
-What do they expect to gain?
-How will this impact decisions down the road?
-What do they want me to do?
-What is the monetary value of what they're offering?

Get really honest with yourself: Are you actually excited about the product, or about the fact that someone is trying to support you?

A great example: A company that made a new kind of protein bar was relentlessly stalking young athletes in my area last year, offering them "sponsorships." The deal was that riders would get some free product and then the riders would be obligated to promote it.

It tempted a lot of riders, but there were a few problems. Let's assess, looking at the previous questions:
1. The product was untested and technically not approved by WADA—it might have been great, but there wasn't any data to back that up.
2. They were approaching pretty much all of the under-23 athletes in the area who raced at a national level
3. They wanted a lot of social media in return for free product in order to boost their sales

4. Having a small nutrition sponsor for some free protein powder would mean riders would have trouble finding other nutrition sponsors

5. They want riders to use social media to promote the brand, but for most of those riders, they already had teams and other sponsors they should have been promoting on social media (and I can add that most of those riders weren't doing a great job even with that!)

6. Protein powder is technically not necessary as a product for racers, and if a racer does want to use it, it's pretty inexpensive to buy from many other sources

7. The protein, to be honest, was kind of gross, and none of the riders approached were currently using it / would buy it if they needed to

Just because someone says that they want to sponsor you doesn't mean you should be saying yes.

In fact, saying NO actually says more about you than adding another logo to your web page. A good sponsor will look at you later and think that you're discerning if you've turned down 'opportunities' like that.

You Don't Need To Be in Every Club

Social media has made the way athletes need to think about sponsorship completely change, and, even as this book is getting written, the social media landscape is changing rapidly. There are two main ways the Wilde quote works: for forms of social media (apps) and for the new way companies are luring "ambassadors" (emphasis on those quotation marks).

For the app side of things:

New types of media come up all the time—offhand, I can remember at least five Instagram-styled platforms that have come and gone in the last few years. Remember Periscope? Neither do most people, but some people really went all in on those videos.

You can test new apps that look exciting, but don't abandon the platform where your audience already is. If you're constantly shifting from one app to another, people won't be able to find you easily, your audience retention will be lower, and you're less likely to amass a large following in any one spot.

Test out new apps and have fun with them if you want to, but stay consistent with the apps that do well.

For 'ambassadors':

The other way we can think about the club accepting you is when it comes to Ambassador Ads on apps like Instagram. You know the ones: they pop up and tell you that X company is looking for new ambassadors JUST LIKE YOU and here's how you can apply.

This is very similar to the previous chapter on the sketchy 'sponsors' that want to give you free crap in exchange for your soul. If a brand is coming to you and deep down, you know you don't have pro-level results yet, be very wary of what they're offering.

And when it comes to applying for ambassador roles, a general rule of thumb is that if a brand is advertising (actually paying to sponsor posts/ ads) on social media that they're looking for ambassadors, it's likely not a great deal for you. It's one thing if the brand announces on their social media that they've opened up sponsorship applications for the season, but if a brand needs to pay to put an ad in front of you about their ambassador program, be wary.

If a brand really wants you as an ambassador and isn't just going to give you a crappy discount or factory seconds from their stash, they'll seek you out one-on-one. Those ads are essentially just cheap marketing tactics, luring you into thinking you're part of something greater, when really, the companies are just marking up their prices and then offering everyone that same 20% off.

A seasoned pro knows that being an 'ambassador' to 25 companies isn't nearly as useful as being sponsored by one solid company. Being a brand ambassador can be a great thing—just try to rationally look at what the company is offering, why they're offering it, and what they can do for you. Some companies have wonderful ambassador programs, and those small-scale ambassador-ships can turn into sponsorships eventually. But most of the time, you're just another cog in their wheel.

Don't Cheat on Sponsors

I mean, don't cheat at all. Duh. But seriously. I was chatting with shop owner and he told me his biggest pet peeve is sponsored athletes who buy gear from other places. This is a common issue, especially for smaller pro-deal sponsorships versus freebies. For example, if a local bike shop sponsors you and you get a steep discount, that means you should be buying everything, from tubes to gels to bikes, there—unless another sponsor (that the shop knows about) is providing them.

Yeah, yeah, I know there are some great deals to be found online, and maybe the shop doesn't carry your favorite brand.

But guess what? If you enter into a sponsorship agreement with that shop, it doesn't matter that they don't carry your favorite brand. You agreed to the sponsorship, that was the deal. If you don't like what the shop carries, don't go into business with them. That's like having a girlfriend, and making out with another girl because you didn't like your girlfriend's taste in nail polish. It's rude, offensive, and will get your ass kicked.

The only exception to this comes when you actively ask a current sponsor, like a shop, if it's OK if you get something from somewhere else. I've seen that work plenty of times, and especially if it's something that wouldn't compete directly with the shop's inventory, it's been fine.

Why does this matter for sponsors? Take this shop owner's point: If a sponsored athlete wants a certain brand of bike frame that the shop doesn't carry in the shop and elects to buy it online, this is problematic in two major ways for the shop:

1. That athlete is no longer helping promote what the bike shop carries in terms of frames, so what use is the athlete? If the athlete isn't riding something that can be bought at the shop, how is the shop supposed to use any photos/videos/etc. of him?

2. The message the athlete is now sending is even worse than if he wasn't

sponsored at all: What he's saying with this other brand of bike frame is that, "I could have gotten one of the frames my sponsor carries for free, but I think they're crappy and I don't want to ride one even if it costs me nothing."

Yeah, I would be annoyed if I was that shop owner.

I see this a ton with young riders: They casually burn sponsors without even thinking about it, and that kind of behavior really stacks up against them. I remember specifically one kid who raced on a team that paid for his bikes and components, which were all Shimano. That year, SRAM, Shimano's main rival, made a run of trucker caps with the SRAM logo on them that—for whatever reason—became the trendy thing to wear, if you were lucky enough to score one. And this kid? He finagled one at a race, and started wearing it all the time. Which, as many people pointed out, made very little sense since nothing he owned or raced was SRAM, but he persisted.

The next year, he was let go from the team—for a few reasons, but mostly, he was fired over a hat. (And no, SRAM did not pick him up.)

Even if you're burning the sponsor in favor of a potential new one, think about this: How is the new sponsor going to feel knowing that you burned someone else for them? Do you think they'll assume you have any loyalty towards them? Probably not, right? So they'll always be a little suspicious of you, and that will work against you in the long run.

As a preventative measure, make a spreadsheet of everything that you're currently getting in terms of sponsorships and deals, even the smallest ones. If it's a bike shop or a business, don't just write the name, list the terms of your deal. That way, you have a good idea of what your current obligations are, so you don't accidentally end up in hot water after promoting a cricket protein when you're sponsored by a shop that pushed whey protein and gives that to you for free.

Additionally, after you've made the list, if something isn't clear, like you're not sure what exactly your deal with a shop is, this is a great time to reach out to the owners and get some clarification about what they expect from you and what you get in return. It may feel awkward to have this discussion but it's worth it.

Junior Considerations: Developmental Opportunities

As a younger rider—usually still in the junior or U23 category—you may be missing out on opportunities that are available from your regional/state/national cycling governing body. You might not realize how many 'projects' are offered to young riders, relatively inexpensively, that can bring you to training camps and big races.

In cyclocross, for instance, USA Cycling has a project for young racers to go to Europe to race the Christmas Week World Cups and secondary races. That offers great experience, potential for prize money, and the chance to showcase your talents to big teams looking for new riders.

Cycling Canada offers similar, and many of the provinces in Canada have cycling organizations that plan trips to races and training camps as well.

Often, the trips won't be free—you'll usually pay a fee plus the airfare—but if you can swing it, it's worth the price to garner that experience if you're already putting up great results in local races and looking to get on a bigger team. And it's almost always much cheaper than putting together a camp or race campaign solo, especially when it comes to handling logistics and—in some sports—mechanic support.

The opportunities tend to not be very well-publicized, so reach out to local and national governing bodies and ask if they have anything coming up if you can't find any camps in an online search.

Going on these camps/projects can be a huge help in securing teams or sponsors for a few reasons.

1. You gain skills and fitness from working with the coaches
2. You gain race experience plus tactical advice from coaches
3. Coaches often have sponsor-related connections and if they like you and see potential, they can help with some hook-ups and intros
4. Coaches from these camps can write letters of reference for you
5. Often, pros will come in and out of these camps, joining in for rides or crashing for a night in the smaller disciplines like cyclocross or MTB, so you gain great access to the highest level of the sport (and often, their managers as well)
6. You might end up with some big results!

Sounds great, right? It really is—and it's shocking how few young racers are aware of these opportunities. Many of the smaller camps aren't even that hard to get onto—you just need to know what races you need to do in order to apply.

So, if you are a young rider, do some searches for national, regional and local programs—if you can't find anything (really look first!!), then email the head coach/director there.

Keeping a Sponsor Happy

A good sponsorship, as I've said many times already, is one where both parties feel like they're getting more than they bargained for. In a happy sponsorship, you're getting amazing levels of support and they're getting tons of publicity and exposure plus some research and development as you use their gear. And even better, both parties feel like there's a real connection. Those are the relationships that continue on beyond one year with a team.

I've seen a lot of athletes switch between teams over the years, and the ones who are best known for good personality as well as their stellar race results are the ones who have sponsors that follow them from team to team. A great example of a sponsor that will pivot with you is Red Bull. The company sponsors athletes in all types of sports, and rather than sponsor any one team, they sponsor a handful of individuals, and they move with them as they shift from team to team, or add/subtract other sponsors. Those are the relationships you want to develop! (And it's not just Red Bull—there are plenty of bike companies that will sponsor entire teams in order to maintain their relationship with a single rider.)

And a great sponsorship helps you prepare for the future, for life after racing. A good sponsor who stays on can even potentially stay with you long after your racing career is over, allowing you to either do more fun runs/rides/shows as a sort of brand mascot, or to shift into a job within the company itself.

"When a sponsorship goes great, it goes beyond business. People who make real relationships stay on teams longer than their performance maybe should allow," says one marketing manager.

But how do you do that, other than by getting the results that sponsors are hoping you'll achieve?

Start by making sure that you're hitting on the specifics outlined in your contract: That might just mean wearing XY Brand t-shirt after every race, it might mean a certain number of social media posts or guest rides. Know what you've signed on for and deliver on it.

But don't stop there. Make space and time for sponsors throughout your season. "I sometimes travel with the team or individual athletes. The best experience is to finish off a block of racing or event and debrief, decompress, and share a meal," says one former team manager. "The best athletes recognize that staff and sponsors go through some degree of the same highs and lows during actual competition. It's important for everyone to bookend that block or season, separating it from what comes next."

It may be more tempting to hit the club with your contemporaries, but I've seen time and time again that the riders who take sponsors to dinner after a National Championship, for example, and hang with them as late as the sponsors are willing to stay out are the ones who get re-signed for the next year, or get job offers post-retirement. (And if the party isn't still raging once dinner is over, the party wasn't that great anyway and you didn't miss much. Trust me on this.)

So while you might feel a bit of FOMO if you're stuck schmoozing sponsors instead of doing shots with your fellow racers, consider it a longterm strategy and think of it as a privilege, not a dirty assignment that you're stuck doing.

Pro tip: Don't wait for a sponsor to suggest something like this—be proactive and suggest grabbing a coffee after a race, bring a cookie or an espresso to a sponsor when you know he or she is at the course. (And if you do get a dinner invite, or a sponsor agrees to a dinner, while it's likely he or she will pick up the tab, don't expect it—be prepared to pay for dinner and know that it's money well-spent.)

"Not every rider is going to get that one-on-one connection with a sponsor," adds that manager. So when you have the opportunity to snag that alone time, take it.

"There's a good new bike racer every day," he says. "And at the end of the day, they're going to be replaced. The ones that stand apart are the ones that left a mark in other ways."

He's reminding us of one very important thing here: careers as athletes do have to end, and will end much earlier than a career at any other corporation will. Not to mention, you may end up on the injured list or need to take time off for some other reason. If you haven't made that intimate connection with a sponsor, the odds of him or her supporting you through a recovery period, or giving you a job after you've left the world of racing, get much slimmer.

So, to stay relevant long after your best racing years are over or to be the one picked for promotional campaigns, kept on teams, and given one-off sponsorships when the company stops working with your team as a whole, start asking yourself these questions: "How well can you be integrated with the brand? How willing are you to work with some level of orchestration? How well do you know the product?"

Figure out the best ways that you can integrate with whatever sponsors you do have, and make it a point to share those ideas: that might mean hosting running shop trail runs or informational shop nights. It might be as simple as wearing the company's casual clothing, or it might mean using Instagram stories or your blog to talk about your favorite ways of using a certain protein powder.

And don't just brainstorm the obvious ones: "We've done some things around charity angles and gotten riders involved to tell the story through their channels," says one manager. What charities or causes are you passionate about? Ellen Noble is a great example of a rider who is known not just for her fantastic results, she's known for her outspoken views on feminism, and her campaigns to get young girls riding. Companies love her and want to help her reach those goals—and, of course, help her ride fast.

Pro tip: After every season, make sure you're sending thank you cards (preferably real cards versus email) with a photo or two (signed) from the season, and even a signed jersey, to your sponsors. (Holiday cards are also a smart move.)

Brainstorm a few outside-the-box ways that you can help your sponsors or make yourself top-of-mind. That might mean just planning to swing by the local shop that you ride for more often, or offering to host a ride. It might be a big charity ride that you'd love to run or take part in.

APPLYING FOR TEAMS + SPONSORSHIPS

The Best Time to Look for a Team

When I first started this chapter, I had intentions of making a full list with a massive table, but the more I chatted with coaches and managers, the more I realized that there isn't one specific time in any sport to apply for a team or sponsorship. There are, however, some general guidelines for the right and wrong times.

The Right Time
The rough guide is this: About mid-way through one race season, you should be thinking about next season and, if you do want to switch teams, you can start making connections with other team owners and managers and quietly sending out your resume. This is also a good time to approach your current team or sponsors about the next year.

If you're already under contract with sponsors, when you're about 6 months from the end of that contract, that's a great time to connect and open discussions for what's next. By the time your season's Nationals or Worlds rolls around, I guarantee you teams for the following season are almost entirely decided upon.

Honestly, it's never too early to telegraph your intentions. Making a contact at a race or sending a preliminary email can be done anytime of year—let a team or potential sponsor know that you're interested in working with them, and ASK when the application should go in, and if they have any specifications for it. At least this way, the conversation has started.

There is one addendum to that: Before you cold-email a company about sponsorship or a team about joining them, check the website for information on applying. Most teams don't have that information available, but nothing will get you ignored faster than if you ignore their clearly stated process.

Pro tip: mention in your email that you looked for this information online and couldn't find it. That way, if they DO have it and you missed it, you just look bad at googling. If they don't have it, they appreciate that you took the time to peruse their site and search for it.

The Wrong Time
The worst time to start chatting with a team about sponsorship is after you've signed a contract with another team. It's bad practice to jump ship or dump sponsors who've already committed to you, so unless the deal is 10 times better and another team is truly a significant upgrade, or your current team is actually treating you like $hit, don't abandon a team.

Note: if you think your team is treating you poorly, write out exactly what's going on, and ask someone experienced for their take on it. What you perceive as poor treatment might just be abruptness or a personality mismatch or you might not be pulling your weight. But if someone else agrees that the behavior of your team is crappy, get out of that situation and, if necessary, report it to the proper authorities or governing bodies.

The day your contract expires is the other worst time to start looking. It might technically be the first day you can actively approach other companies, but you should have already been planning and making connections long before this point. Waiting until this point puts you in the defensive position of not having anything in place and scrambling, and makes you more likely to accept whatever is being offered.

How to Find
Your Contact

Start with Google
The worst thing you can do? Not Google around for an email address of the marketing person or sponsorship coordinator at a company. As the previous chapter reminds us, it's the most irritating thing for a sponsorship coordinator to get an email asking about the application process or with a racer resume when there's a page with application information on the brand's website.

Check LinkedIn
Do a deep dive into who works at the company—LinkedIn is an amazing resource for this, and will often have contact info.

Check Your Specific Media
In cycling, Bicycle Retailer or Pinkbike often posts press releases about new teams and riders that have quotes from sponsorship/marketing managers at the companies. This is a great way to find the names of the people who you want to reach out to.

Ask Your Circle (Privately)
Reach out to friends and acquaintances who work for or with the companies you're hoping to make contact with. Often, just asking your well-connected friends if they know anyone at company X will give you at least a lead on a contact, if not an introduction.

A Few Tips Around Sending Emails

The next section in this book is cover-letter-specific, but after spending more time with young racers (and some more seasoned ones!), I realized that we needed to also talk about emailing in general. So, before we dive into the sponsor-specifics, let's get general about your email communication:

Have a reasonable email address
Your name should be in it. Something like FastRacer69@yahoo.com is no longer cool. (Really, was it ever?) A Gmail or whatever service provider you use is fine, but stick to your name, i.e JohnSmith@gmail.com. If you get an email address with your website (i.e john@johnsmith.com) that's great, but it's not necessary.

... And a reasonable signature
This doesn't need to be fancy, but pertinent contact info is much more appreciated than a crazy quote. Name, email, phone, and any relevant web-pages/social links like a personal website, Twitter, etc.

Write your email outside of your email program
This helps avoid the "oh crap, I hit Send too fast" mid-email mess up. If this is a pain in the ass, just write your body text and the subject line before putting the email address in the To field.

Use Google Docs/Word
On that note, typing your email in one of these solves your typing-emails-outside-of-email issue, and provides better spellcheck than Gmail or Yahoo Mail provide.

Try Grammarly

This free app (available at https://www.grammarly.com) is great for the grammar-confused among us. It does a final check in Gmail, scanning your email for common grammar mistakes.

Did you check the attachments?

No lie, I've gotten hideously inappropriate images attached to emails (yikes…) that were supposed to have rider card images attached. That's because on the other side, someone didn't check which file they attached before hitting send. Please, please, please check that.

Don't attach massive files

Not only can these send you right to spam, they take forever to download so most people will just skip downloading them altogether. Use a resize tool (on a Mac, use Preview and export to JPG as low-quality or download the free JPEGmini Lite app; on a PC, simply take a screenshot of your high-res photo for the fastest resize).

Name your attachments properly

The aforementioned mistake is easy to avoid if you name attachments, and the person on the other end will thank you. I download files constantly and just as constantly lose them because I have no freaking idea what the person named it. Images, resumes, docs… just a simple, clear name is super helpful.

Really, did you check the attachments?

The other mistake I see (and have made) a ton is saying "see attachment" and then forgetting to actually attach the image. Again, just double-check. Best bet: attach things before you even start writing the email!

Crushing the Application Process

OK, the scary part: applications. Sometimes, a company will have an easy-to-fill out form online. But those are few and far between, and I've noticed that the companies and teams that do offer that tend to be lower-level ambassador-style programs versus legit paying teams. So most likely, you're emailing an application to someone at the company.

Tell them what you're applying for
I recently heard about a racer who got skipped from the Nationals team, not because he wasn't qualified—he was—and not because he forgot to apply—he did—but because nowhere in his application email did he actually say what he was applying for! So, while it might have been obvious in the moment to him, for the manager looking through applications (likely by doing a simple search on his Gmail), this application didn't get picked up and the racer was ignored.

Have a clean, up-to-date resume
We'll get into the resume itself in a second, but even before the application process starts, have your resume ready to go—and every couple months, check and update it!

Know your timelines
While some teams and sponsors have pretty open-ended applications, some companies and teams are specific about when they're going to be accepting applications. Know those dates, and note them in your calendar. If a company has an application window, unless you're a Gold medalist or World Champ, your application is getting ignored if you get it in late.
Know what they want

Some companies and teams are specific about what an application should look like. Some want resumes, some want essays, some are looking for someone who's got a great social media presence and some are looking for results. Try to get a sense of what they want—they'll either tell you on an application page, or they'll show you if you just look up athletes who are currently sponsored by them.

Follow them
Before you hit Send, follow the companies you're interested in on social media. Follow athletes who are sponsored by that company, and—assuming their profiles are public, not set to private—consider following some of the people who work at the company. Not only will this potentially put you on their radar, it gives you a bit of insight into the personalities that surround that company. And if they do dig into your application and stalk you on social media, they'll see that you're following the company and actually care about it.

Get ready for rejection
Sorry, guys. Rejection is just part of the pro athlete game. Don't expect responses to every application that you send, and don't expect everyone to love you. If you can be OK with this before you hit SEND, you'll be a lot better off.

Get organized
Start looking over that list of teams/sponsors that you're interested in. Research each one, seeing if there is an application time period. If there is, note it on the calendar. Make a spreadsheet of each company/team, key contact person, their contact info, their position, the website with any application info, and anything that the company notes it's looking for.

Writing a Cover Letter (or Cover Email)

When you're writing to someone about sponsorship, unless you're best friends or siblings, assume that the person you're messaging doesn't know you. Or, if they do know you, assume that they'll appreciate a gentle reminder. People reading these applications get a ton from other racers, so even if Person A at Company X knows you and you two chat a ton at races, Person A might not actually know your name, or be able to match that name to the face.

This isn't the cover letter that you worked on perfecting back in high school. Today's cover letters are a) emails, and b) in the fitness/wellness sphere, a little bit more unbuttoned than if you were applying for an internship at a hedge fund.

"Send a mini-dek—your quick pitch—via email," says one team manager. "You know, 'Hi, John, I'm so and so.' If I'm doing my job, I already know you if you're good, but still say who you are, what you're about, a bit about your racing and history." And yes, you'll attach your race resume so putting some race results here might seem a bit extra, but remember that you need to get the person on the other end interested enough to actually open it!

If you have a personal note ('It was great drinking espresso with you after Tour of XY,') this is a great spot to add that as a reminder.

Even if you don't have that personal contact, know who you're sending the letter to—definitely get the company right, but if you can actually address it to a person, even better. "Make it personalized," he added. "I've seen it happen where someone sent me something with other brands and names in it. Be careful not to send spam letters.

This is potentially your first contact with the brand—even if it isn't, pretend that it is. "It's like trying to get any job," he added. "You're making a first impression."

Here's how to make that first impression count—assuming that the company hasn't put out specific guidelines for their application process. You're aiming for something that's readable in 90 seconds or less.

A well-written subject line
The main difference in cover letter writing compared to what you learned as a kid is that the subject line becomes as important as the body of your email. Clearly state what sponsorship you're looking for, your name, and—if it makes sense—a short descriptor of yourself, i.e 'Junior road race national champion.'

A polite, correctly spelled greeting
Please, please, please check how the person you're writing to spells his or her name. And use a name, never "to whom it may concern." (True story: the former editor-in-chief of Bicycling, after I'd been there for three years, pulled up an email pitch I had sent him when I was 20 and mocked me for using that phrase.) If you don't know a name, just a simple 'Hello—' is fine.

1-2 sentences "mini-dek"
Who you are, what you're all about, and why you're emailing. Keep this simple, we'll go more in-depth in a second.

1-2 sentences about why you like the team/product/service
If you can't come up with anything, you shouldn't be approaching them in the first place.

1-2 sentences of small talk
"I was so excited when your team member XX had a great result at Worlds," or even simply "I hope you're enjoying some off-season time." This seems overly simplistic, but if really does set a polite tone.

2-3 sentences about your goals for the upcoming season

Similar to the 'objectives' section of a race resume: "I'm planning to race more in Europe next season and I'm looking for a team that will support my efforts as a U23." Include pertinent details, i.e nationality if that's not obvious, and age/level (U23, elite male, etc.).

Your query

Something like "I was wondering if you're looking for any new team members/sponsored athletes this season?" or "I'm hoping you'll consider me for the XY team."

2-3 sentences with race resume highlights, in context

Sure, they can open the attachment to see your whole resume, but why should they? Give them a couple reasons. ("I was junior national champion last year, and after a few European races where I scored top 20 spots, I wanted to focus more on racing there.) Mention that the PDF resume is attached for them to check out.

Add links / any metrics

If you mention your Instagram, list your follower count and link it. Blog? Link it. It's extremely annoying for someone to have to search for your Instagram if you mention you have 50,000 followers and they want to check you out. Make it easy, and it'll get clicked. Make it hard, and it'll get passed over.

1-2 sentences thanking them for their time

Mention that even if they aren't looking for new riders, it would be great to even have a phone call with the manager/team development person to possibly get some tips on improving and being able to find a team for the next year. (This will be the best rejection phone call you could possibly hope for, because you'll learn A TON.)

Email like an adult

Don't use emojis. Think conversation with a manager at work, not chatting on Tinder. And again, SPELL CHECK.

A reasonable, polite signature

Sincerely, Cheers, et cetera. and your full name. Under that, include a signature that has: phone, email, website/Twitter/instagram (if applicable) so that the addressee can take a quick look at you.

ATTACH YOUR FREAKING RESUME!

Seriously, don't hit send before you attach that PDF. And make sure it's named so that it's easy to find once it's downloaded, i.e Mary-Smith-Race-Resume.PDF. (I've gotten so many emails in recent years that come with a follow-up five minutes later saying "Oh, and here's the attachment I forgot." I have also sent emails like this. It happens to everyone, so if you do forget, a polite, apologetic email with the attachment helps.)

Attach your letter in a PDF format

Some managers collect potential athlete information in a folder some-where on their computer, so make it even easier for them by creating a PDF version of your cover letter (in Microsoft Word or using Canva online to make its bit fancier) and name it appropriately, then attach along with your resume. It's a small extra step but it can make a difference.

Tailoring Your Race Resume

To be honest, resumes are kind of a drag. But hey, it's part of the pro athlete game.

Most sponsors freaking hate reading race resumes—especially boring, poorly put together ones that are one-dimensional. Basically, a race resume will only get you so far. But you will need one for these applications, so let's talk.

"Your progression stands out on your race resume," says one brand manager, so make sure yours is telling a cohesive story. Don't drop Junior results as soon as you age out, just pick-and-choose the best ones. But make sure that there's an obvious progressive trend of getting better/faster/smarter/stronger throughout. When you're putting one together, here are a few simple tips:

One. Page.
It's tempting to include EVERYTHING, but keep it to a single page. Most sponsors won't look past the first page anyway, honestly.

Include Your Contact Info and Internet Persona
Name, email, address, phone number, Twitter/Instagram handles and (if you have one), racer website should all be at the top. Keep this simple!

Keep It Clean
Obviously, keep your language clean. But also keep the look of the page clean and simple. An single image of you racing (that you have rights to) is great, but don't make a collage. Don't use Comic Sans or other "fun"

fonts. Use a free site like canva.com, which has free templates that look great, to make your PDF.

Seriously, a PDF

Don't mess around with Word docs, where formatting can vary from computer to computer. Take the two seconds and make your resume into a PDF (there are tons of free sites for this, and again, canva.com will do that for you!). You can include it in the body of an email as well (with your cover letter), but attaching a nicely laid-out PDF is the smart move.

Pick a Few Key Results

When you put it together, don't list every. single. race. you've done this season. Pick a couple of key results to highlight (and you can always add a link to a page on your website where you list the entire race season's results).

Spell (and Grammar) Check!

Sponsors are looking for sloppiness: if you can't be professional and do a quick check of your resume, what will you do once you're actually on a team? Spellcheck is such a no-brainer in this day and age that skipping it makes you look like an enormous putz.

Side note: I'm a huge, huge proponent of consistent capitalization and I see TONS of resumes that skip between world cup and World Cup and World cup and it drives me bananas. Just stick to one format for things like that and it will read a lot cleaner.

Include Some Hobbies

Racers like Jeremy Powers are well known for their awesome racing ability, of course, but they also have distinguished themselves with other talents—in Jeremy's case, his love of DJing. That hobby allows sponsors to plan more unique events with him, and that's helped endear him to his sponsors and to the public. You don't have to turn tables to make yourself sale-able, but if you love writing (or already keep a great blog), or you enjoy playing guitar, or you crush it at Ultimate Frisbee, that makes you more memorable, and potentially gives sponsors ideas on ways to use you in promotion outside of riding your bike really, really fast.

Add a Photo

Sure, they can look you up on Instagram, but it's nice to give people an idea of who you are—and it humanizes you. (As per previous chapters, make sure you have the photo rights to the one you use.)

Update Yearly
And check the years. In the race resumes I've edited, I'd say 75 percent of them have info from last year, or new objectives but last year's dates listed with them. Check in after every season and tweak goals, results and even your bio: things that were true last year may not be the same, and you may find you want to add different facts/highlights, or change your photo.

Note Current Sponsors/Teams
Mention who you're currently supported by to a) establish credibility, and b) note the dates of when you'll be free to be sponsored by other companies. And make sure if you have some independent sponsors already lined up, they're mentioned as well—the last thing a brand wants to do is sign on to work with you only to find you're also repping a brand that the new sponsor has a problem with.

Stick to That Single Page
Seriously. Any more than that gets tedious for sponsors—and honestly, hard to remember everything. The more you put, the more it all blurs together.

Name It Properly
Your-name-athlete-resume.pdf. It's that simple. My greatest pet peeve is getting resumes that just are named 'racer resume.pdf, because it means I can't easily find Sally Smith's if I'm looking for it.)

JANE SMITH

ULTRA-DISTANCE TRAIL RUNNER
INSTAGRAM: @JANESMITH87

2020 OBJECTIVES

To top-5 at Leadville 100-miler
Win Northface Endurance Challenge 50-miler at Bear Mtn NY
Continue to share my journeys on my website, janesmithrunning.com
Find a set of sponsors who will support my development as an athlete

CONTACT INFORMATION

Cell: (123) 456 7890
Home: (123) 456 7890
Email: hello@reallygreatsite.com
Website: www.janesmithrunning.com
Instagram: JaneSmith87

ABOUT ME

I'm a 27-year-old endurance runner based in New York City, and I've loved running since I was 12 years old and joined my school's cross-country team. Since then, I graduated college with a degree in English and raced cross-country for two seasons before injuries forced me to take a break from competitive racing. But since then, I've come back and fallen in love with ultra-running—when I'm not working on my novel or teaching yoga classes.

RACE RESULTS

2nd, 2019 XYZ Endurance Challenge 50K NY
5th, 2019 XYZ Race 50 miler VT
3rd, 2018 XYZ Mountain Run 50K VT
5th, 2018 2nd, 2019 XYZ Endurance Challenge 50K TX
7th, 2018 XYZ Race 50 miler NC
3rd, 2017 XYZ Mountain Run 50K VT
5th, 2016 XYZ Race 50 miler CA

CURRENT SPONSORS

Random hydration company (ending 2020)
Random clothing company (though 2021)
Random yoga studio in town (through 2023)

The Art of the Follow-Up

The art of the follow up is important for a few situations: When you've applied to a team or for a project and haven't heard back, when waiting to hear from sponsors, or even when you're waiting to for an interview with you to be scheduled or published.

What you don't want to do is appear desperate. But you do want to make sure you stay on the radar if you're trying to work with your dream team. So if you don't hear back, here's how you can gently follow-up.

Wait AT LEAST Two Weeks
As a reporter—and as a team manager who's gotten a lot of questions from riders looking for a spot on the team—I can tell you that my biggest pet peeve is when someone emails 24 hours later to ask if I received his email. Sorry, but assume that answering you isn't someone's top priority and give them at least two weeks before enacting any of these tips. The caveat to the two week rule is applications with due dates. Give those at least a month, since most of the time, the company won't get to them immediately. And definitely don't follow up until after the due date has gone by!

Plan Ahead for Follow-Ups
On your calendar where you've listed application dates/when you're going to send cover letters to each, make follow-up notes for 2 to 4 weeks after each one. It's a great way to keep track of/remind yourself where you're at with each. A spreadsheet for this (the one you made to keep track of how to apply) is ideal: add a column for date sent, and one for a followup, plus

one for notes on how the process is going/any communications.

Do Make Sure Your Email Sent
This is a hugely embarrassing one. Sometimes, your phone or computer glitches and a message gets stuck in Drafts instead of Sent. So before you start thinking about the follow-up, check your Sent folder and make sure that the email has gone out—and check to make sure you sent it to the correct email address. This might sound hard to believe, but I've had it happen and made a complete ass out of myself.

Start Unobtrusively
If you're dealing with a reporter or a smaller-scale sponsor, a great tactic is to make sure you're following them on social media, and replying to or liking their (relevant) posts. A personal story: I was featuring a young woman on one of my sites and the story got bumped back (this happens often, especially when you're not dealing with time-sensitive material). She didn't email to ask what the deal was or when she could expect to see the story; instead, she started commenting on different posts that I was sharing on social media. She didn't mention her interview, just enthusiastically joined the conversations. Not only did I publish her story the next week, she also made her way onto my regular rotation of favorite pros to talk to.

Follow-Up, Once
Send a polite follow-up email a couple weeks after the first one. Remember, most people aren't trying to be rude, they're just busy. (Pro trick: I write my emails like these while smiling and pretending I'm writing to a good friend. It's easy to accidentally come off more aggressive than you plan to be and seem demanding, so really focus on keeping your tone friendly.) Rather than asking if someone saw your last email, mention it, but add something of value: "I wrote this new blog post I thought you'd be interested in," "Check out this Instagram photo," et cetera. And end by asking if there's any other info you can provide. Ending on a question is a sneaky move because then etiquette dictates that it requires a response.

Switch Your "To" Field
After the second follow-up fails, it's time to look for another way to reach your target. That means looking for a new person to email, which could mean a horizontal move within the company. For example, you've been talking to the communications director of a sunglasses company, but now

you can try to email the social media director. Look for similar job titles. (Sometimes even sending your original message to the more generic info@ email address can get it in the right hands.) Basically, don't keep bugging the same person when you're not getting a response. Remember the definition of insanity: doing the same thing over and over and expecting different results.

Leave (Personal) Facebook Out of It When Possible
If someone has a professional page, by all means, feel free to message them on that. But for journalists and people who work for a company you're hoping will sponsor you, leave those poor people alone on Facebook/Instagram unless their page actually says commercial inquiries are welcome. Speaking from personal experience, I can't stand when people message me on there for work, unless that's where we've already had a conversation. And it's even more annoying for someone who doesn't have any actual power in the company and is just trying to use her Facebook at home to communicate with friends and gets your message asking why Red Bull isn't sponsoring you.

Rule of Three
Sometimes, you won't hear back. And while you shouldn't necessarily keep pestering a potential sponsor over and over, a follow-up email a couple weeks later is fine, and one more after that. Just don't get obsessive about it. Like romantic connections, if someone is interested, they will be in touch. A gentle nudge is fine, but if you keep pushing after two follow-ups, you're torching your chances to ever work with that company.

Didn't Work? Think Laterally
If a company didn't answer you, consider looking for a company doing equally cool stuff. If that doesn't work, zoom out and think outside the box. Is there a local shop that stocks the sunglasses company that you were hoping to score, and could they sponsor you instead?

The Art of the Interview

10

Most sponsors or teams will want to at least speak to you on the phone, if not in real life. While I'm not going to dig in too deep on what to say, there are a few general things worth noting before you pick up the phone or go into a meeting.

In general:
—Be yourself. That's the main piece of advice here. Don't try to sell yourself like you're a used car dealer, or make wild claims about races you're going to win in the future. Just act as normal as possible, be interested in the company or the team, be respectful, and be polite.
—Be on time. Enough said. (Be super aware of this for phone interviews where time zones may be an issue.)
—Have a few talking points ready. Be yourself, but always have a plan! Make a few notes ahead of the meeting, like certain makes/models/colors that the company does that you really liked this season. Refresh yourself on your racing objectives and resume, and brainstorm a fun or funny anecdote from the season. That way, you won't get caught off-guard.
—Have a few questions you want to ask them. Most interviewers end with 'do you have any questions for us' and it's nice to be able to ask one—and as an interviewer, I can tell you that it makes us feel like you've really done your homework. It can be a question about the company, about a specific product, or even just about what happens next.
 —If it's your first interview, consider asking a parent or coach to do a mock interview with you beforehand to prep and get rid of the jitters.
—Afterwards, don't head to social media to talk about the interview. Play it cool.

—The next day, send a thank you email. This serves two purposes. First, it's polite, and people notice things like that. But second, it reminds the person about your interview and puts you back in their inbox.

On the phone:
—Know who's phoning who, at what time, which time zone, and at what number.
—Make sure your phone's volume is on so you don't miss the call.
—Check that you have good service and a quiet area to speak. I've ended up sweating in my van on calls because I misjudged how quiet a cafe would be!
—Have a glass of water on hand. Sounds silly, but you may end up with dry mouth if you're nervous on phones. You don't want to make a lot of rustling noise during this call, so having the glass of water ready saves you from getting one!
—Use a pen and paper to take notes—people can hear typing over the phone and it's annoying.

In person:
—Have the address in your GPS and have a plan for parking. Leave a buffer of time to get there so you don't end up sprinting to a building!
—Bring note-taking material, no one wants to see you typing away on your phone when they're talking to you.
—Silence your phone when you get there.
—Assume the dress code is business casual, but on the casual end. Dress like you would going to a decent restaurant: As an athlete, you have some leeway, but showing up in your athletic gear is generally frowned upon.
—Bring a copy of your resume, it saves them time. This is also a good chance to bring any print journalism about you, if you've been in a magazine or newspaper.
—Be polite to everyone. This should sound obvious, but it's worth repeating because I've seen young athletes act like entitled jerks when talking to secretaries or receptionists. Treat everyone in the building with the utmost respect.

At a race:
A lot of interviews happen at races, which sounds convenient but can pose some serious challenges. You're likely tired and sweaty, in addition to being stressed about your race performance and interview performance. Here's what you need to remember:

—Look as professional as possible. In these cases, athletic clothing is perfectly fine, you'd look weird in a business suit. But make sure your face/body are wiped down, you've swiped on some deodorant, and you've checked that you don't still have mud between your teeth.

—Hydrate and snack post-race. No one wants to deal with a fainting athlete, and hanger can set in if you're not careful!

—Know who you're meeting. I've seen so many athletes fumble into tents where they have meetings, only to forget the name of the person they're meeting with. It's a lot to deal with post-race, but check your phone quickly before the meeting and confidently ask to speak to that person when you get to the tent.

—Silence your phone.

—Prepare for it to be awkward as well as ultra-casual. Once you're in the meeting, a lot of team managers and sponsorship coordinators plan these meetings at races, but are then inundated with other requests, people swinging by to just say hello, et cetera. Assume that it's going to be a bit of a cluster, and remain calm and positive.

—Bring your resume. A printed copy can be really helpful when someone forgot to download yours and the service in the area sucks.

—Mirror the interviewer. If he's sitting and there's a chair, sit. If he's standing, stay standing. If he's wearing sunglasses, you can keep yours on, otherwise, take them off. These things sound minor but send strong messages.

GETTING TO KNOW THE WORLD OF SPORT: TEAM DYNAMICS + MEDIA

Know Where
True Power Lies

As the racer, it can be tempting to see people in supporting roles as 'the little people.' It might be tempting to blow off an interview request, snap at a mechanic, or complain about a promoter on Twitter. Bad moves—remember that Golden Rule from the beginning of this book? That doesn't just apply to friends/family/teammates. That applies to a lot of people who you might not think have huge roles in your sport, but who can make or break your sponsorships.

Here are a few of the classic people who often get mistreated, but who can absolutely influence your career. Treat them right, and you'll be much, much happier and infinitely more successful.

Note: I don't mean that you should be a condescending, saccharine sweet pain-in-the-ass to these guys. I've seen a lot of young racers do that, and it comes off schmoozy, obnoxious, and incredibly obvious. Be your pleasant self, and just remember that you're all at work—your job descriptions are just a bit different.

And this applies even when one of these people is kind of being a dick (which does happen often). You're not going to get anywhere by being equally dick-ish back, just be as polite as possible and don't engage rather than starting a fight. Upper management and fellow racers see this and the more polite you are, the better you look in any interaction. Make a note of altercations and absolutely talk to upper management if someone is being rude to you. Advocate for yourself, but try to avoid starting drama 10 minutes before a race unless it's an emergency or unlivable situation.

With that said, here are just a few of the people you should remember can make or break your career:

Mechanics

Ever had a last minute repair you needed right before a race that was done perfectly, or scored a bonus set of wheels or tires from a friendly mechanic? Yeah, being nice to your local shops' mechanic or your team's mechanic can pay off big-time. If you're rude or dismissive, I promise you that mechanics do not forget that. In the heat of a race, you might end up screaming at one. My advice? Try not to do that—remember that they're doing their best, and they're likely not at fault for whatever went wrong. If you do freak out mid-race, apologize immediately post-race. And always make sure that after a race, you say thank you. In fact, just say thank you a bunch in general. You might not think that's a big deal, but it is.

Media

Wonder how some racers get into news and training stories more often than others? That's because certain racers are friendlier and easier to get in touch with. Shocker: these are the racers that people in the endurance sport media will gravitate towards for quick-hit answers for stories ranging from race reports to training tip pieces, which sponsors freaking love. If you want to make sure your side of the racing story gets told, or sneak some mentions of favorite products into a nutrition roundup, befriending reporters and journalists—just being polite, answering emails and questions post-race—is the way to go. (I'll tell a story later in here that will make you cringe.)

Photographers

A photographer that you're friendly with is a lot more inclined to snap your photo and send it to a magazine or website when they ask for race images. They're also more willing to give you a deal on buying rights, and that can be hugely helpful.

Commissaires

Sure, commissaires are tasked with following the rules to the letter. But whether they cut you a break and bend them a bit or just shut you down, often depends on how nice you are. (I've seen fines get lifted a few times in my life—and in every case, it was because the racer was well-known as being extremely nice and friendly with the officials.) Don't pander or be obnoxious, just say hello, thank you, et cetera—and smile occasionally!

Promoters

Race promoters are much more likely to let you into events for free or invite you back if you make an effort to befriend them. That might mean bringing some swag they can use for prizes (or swag for them/their families), it might mean a thank you note after a race. It might just mean that you remember his or her name and make an effort to strike up conversation on the race day.

Assistants
When you're working with any company, whether you're an influencer or an athlete, you're likely going to end up emailing or chatting with an assistant of someone you're hoping to get in touch with or get money/product from. First of all, assistants are the gatekeepers. Piss them off and your emails and follow-up calls may not get passed along. (And a president of a company is way more likely to believe his assistant when he says he never heard from you versus you saying you called a few times and that jerk didn't pass on your message!) Secondly, most of those people take their assistants opinions very seriously and don't appreciate their assistants being treated like crap or talked down to. Assume every assistant will one day be your boss and act accordingly.

Soigneurs
Any member of the team, really: from drivers to managers and everyone in between, it pays to stay on their good sides. A lot of gossip happens between team staff, and if you piss off a masseuse, the odds are good he'll complain to the mechanic, and suddenly, you're getting the brush-off from him. And that creeps up the chain to the team director, who gets to decide if you're on the team next year.

Your Teammates
If I've learned one thing in my years in endurance sport, it's that teammates, even ones that you're close with, love to gossip. Try to rise above it, or at least, don't drop any huge bombs. Even if a racer is more junior than you or doesn't have the same great results you do, that could—and probably will—change.

Remember, not all of these people are amazing people. Photographers can be absolute nightmares, mechanics can do crappy work, teammates can be hard to live with—but that's part of life, unfortunately. Most people will tell you that they have awful co-workers. You just have to be able to deal with the crappy people with as much grace as possible.

Think back to a few races. Can you think of any examples of moments where you could have behaved better? Even if you've never been outwardly rude, was there a time you could have made more of an effort to make friendly conversation or even just say thanks? Write down a few examples—not so you can make amends or anything, just to embed it in your brain so that next time, you don't make the same mistake.

A Word On Not Pissing Off Photographers

As a pro athlete trying to build your personal brand, social media is obviously hella important. Equally important, though, is not pissing off or getting sued by photographers, so don't feel free to post just any picture of you.

Some photogs will be super happy to let you post their photo (with proper credits, of course). But others can be prickly about it, so always ask before you post. If you're generally pleasant and thank people for photos and share links to their content, they're more likely to want to help you out. On the flip side, as soon as you burn one photographer by not crediting him and using his photo as your own, the other photographers hear about it. It's a small world.

And yes—some photographers and reporters can be jerks (I say that as one of them. I know from experience). But that doesn't mean you should use their photos and not worry about the backlash.

Sponsors really hate getting caught in the middle of stuff like this, and don't forget: if you post a photo, the sponsor might retweet or re-gram it. If you didn't get the rights to that photo, the sponsor can also get in trouble. And who's the sponsor going to be pissed at? Yep, you.

That all sounds super negative, but it doesn't have to be: plenty of photographers are really friendly if you take the time to reach out, say hello, and (again) ask for permission to re-post photos. Most of them are excited about the exposure / understand that you're not making a ton of money to pay for photo rights either.

Case in point: One racer, we'll call him Don, has been sharing links to different sites and sources for photos for years, all linked and credited. He needed a header image for his website, and his favorite photographer had a great one of him. He reached out, asked, and was given the high-res image with just an ask that he caption it with the photographer's name. (The photographer actually thanked him for always crediting him and linking to his work over the years!)

So, he got a free, great photo for his site.

By contrast, we'll call racer B 'Suzy.' Suzy has been racing for a couple years, but has a habit of Instagramming photos of herself racing that she finds online, sometimes remembering to mention where she got them. Suzy just got an angry letter from that same photographer Don was emailing with, and an invoice for the Instagram use was attached.

Sure, it's a picture of you—in fact, you make the picture. That still, unfortunately, doesn't give you the right to use it.

One last word: if you do ask a photographer for images, and he or she sends them to you, USE them. That photographer spent a lot of time taking the photos and then sending them to you (it's a process). It's extremely rude to make them do that only to not use the photo, so make sure you thank, use and credit when you do get photos. The photographer will stop sending you pictures if you don't use them.

Skim your social media from last season and make sure you haven't stolen any photos. If you have, send an apology to the photographer, and that olive branch might actually serve to help you build a relationship for next season!

The Art of the Online Interview

Why does this matter? Because the better you are at responding to journalists, the more often they'll email to feature you in things outside of race reports. Case in point: I sent a quick email for quotes for a story in a major magazine to 15 junior racers. Three answered immediately, three said they'd get back to me (only one actually did) and the rest either waited a week or didn't respond at all. The three that answered immediately are now regulars that I email for quotes for major articles, which has in turn boosted their social media profiles and (I believe) given them a leg-up on the competition when it came to getting on better teams.

How can you get interviewed more? It starts with making the first interview request you get count. As one racer told me it, "The first time you get interviewed, you're on the clock."

So let's get to work. Here's what you need to know when a writer, podcaster, blogger or photographer emails you asking for help for an article. (This will shift as you become a bigger, more sought after person in the sport. We're talking about right now, when you're trying to grow your following.) These tips are based on a decade of being a race reporter and cycling journalist who's written for every major cycling outlet.

Respond Quickly

I recently did an article on morning routines of fitness experts. I emailed some huge names—we're talking follower counts in the millions—and some lesser-known ones. I was shocked when the biggest names were the first to respond, most of them within the same day. The lesser-known ones had big lag times, and were kind of a pain. I realized that this is why the big names are big: Because they jump at opportunities to gain new fans and followers, and they respect the major media outlets that can give them huge bumps in publicity for free.

Actually Answer in Your Response

When someone emails to say something like, "I'm hoping to get a quick quote from you about XY race," or "about your morning routine," PLEASE RESPOND WITH A QUOTE THAT THEY CAN USE. Do not respond with "sure, what do you need?" or "sure, I'll get you something later.". This is infuriating for journalists because it adds another email to the chain and we often have to bug you again. Answer the first time with something quotable ("Every morning, I try to meditate for 10 minutes because blah blah blah"), and a journalist might come back with a follow-up question. This method guarantees that you get into the article that he or she is working on. I've nixed a lot of riders from my regular "people to ping when I need a quote for a training/nutrition/racing article" list for this exact reason. Be easy to reach and easy to quote.

Remember Race Reports are Time Sensitive

When I file a race report, it's within an hour or two of the race finishing. So I'll be emailing/texting/calling for a quote within 15 minutes of the race being over if I'm not there to ask a question on site. If you want to improve your media presence, check your email after the race and keep an eye on it. Stay in practice by drafting a quick quote after every race that you do—it'll come in handy to use later for your social media or athlete website even if no one asks you for a quote.

Email is Ideal

If you're given the choice of a phone interview or email, opt for email unless you're super comfortable talking on the phone. It gives you a chance to carefully consider what you're going to say, plus slip in references and add links to sponsors and products that might be harder to do over the phone, especially when weird spellings, brand names or product types are involved. Doing in-person interviews is super important, but here's a secret tip: if a journalist is saying "email or phone is great," he or she is probably hoping that you're up for an email answer, because it makes our lives a lot easier. If the journalist really wants that one-on-one phone time, she'll specify phone versus giving you the option.

...But Practice Your Interview Skills

Even if you're talking to a stuffed animal, spend time honing your interview skills. Similar to what I said about writing out quotes post-race, try having a debriefing with a parent or friend about how the race went, pretending that whatever you say will be published. This is hugely valuable especially if you're a little emotional after races (good or bad) and can help you avoid putting your foot in your mouth.

Attach a Photo
Reporters may not ask for them, but having a few rights-free "stock" images of yourself riding (I talk about how to do a photoshoot later—keep a few higher-res ones from that) ready to go. That way, when a magazine or website asks you for one, you don't need to hunt something down, force them to hunt something down, or take a fast sub-par one. You'll already have a folder prepped with your favorites (and this also guarantees that it's a good shot of you!). In an article like 'Race morning secrets of racers,' if you can send a photo along with your quote, it will almost always get used prominently because outlets are always looking for free images.

Have a Bio Ready
Just like the photo folder, have a quick 3-4 sentence bio written up, explaining who you are, where you're from, your current team, recent race results, and any relevant web and social media handles and links. Again, this helps reporters immensely. Just remember: Assume that as reporters, we prefer to be lazy. We don't like doing extra work, especially for newer racers. When you've made it big, your PR guy will handle this step, but for now, help a reporter out. We prefer to chase leads, not current team names.

There is No Such Thing as "Off the Record"
Sure, a journalist can't print something you say 'off the record,' technically. But if you complain about another racer, say something off-color, or just start cursing up a storm, the journalist will remember it. He may not write it, but it will impact his opinion of you, how he writes about you, and how often he writes about you. Added to that, it will almost certainly get passed on to other reporters/friends of the reporter. We swim in a small pool in the endurance sport world. That reporter may end up working for the company that you slammed, or end up becoming friends with the racer that you mentioned you hate. So remember that nothing is truly off-the-record.

There are tons of great articles out there that really highlight smart, dedicated racers who are crushing it for their sponsors: I've even listed a few of my favorites in the Resources section on athletesponsorshipguide.com. Give a couple of the articles a read and see what you can take away from them. Then, test yourself by either faking a set of interview questions about a previous race—especially one that didn't go well—or even enlisting a friend to faux-interview you. (It's better to try an interview over the phone so you learn how to handle that!)

The Post-Race Interview

I have a fun story for you guys. I was at the finish line of a big race a few years ago. Now, this one racer had a rough day. Like, really rough. He should have been in the front of the race, but an early mechanical issue on his bike wrecked his chances.

But the athlete made a good comeback, and as he came into the finishing straight, all the photogs stuck around to take pics and get interviews with him because he pulled off a decent result despite an unfortunate series of events.

He crosses the line, and this guy could have been the story of the day. I was there with my camera, I had been talking to a ton of other journalists. They were all saying the same thing: his comeback was more interesting than anything else in the race, he was the story that they wanted to tell.

This kid rolls through the finish and immediately starts screaming at everyone to, and I quote, "Get the $#CK out of my way!" as he literally barrels through the reporters and photogs who had stuck around to talk to him.

Opportunity missed? Hell yeah. Bridges burned? Oh, for sure. For the rest of that season, reporters thought of him as unapproachable and kind of a jerk.

The day I planned to work on this chapter, I—and I am not making this up—woke up and checked the cycling news feeds. What did I see? One of the top cyclists in the world pitching a freaking fit on the roadside during a race… All captured on video by the media surrounding him. He THROWS his bike and screams the F-word. And this dude makes six figures (at least) to race his bike.

His sponsors? Likely not thrilled. His fans? Disappointed.

Guess what, guys? $hit happens. It happens A LOT in sports that rely on equipment, but it can happen in any type of race. You might get food poisoning, miss an aid station, get a blister for an unknown reason.

Your sponsors don't want you to lie to the press after a bad race, but they do want you to a) not be a dick to reporters, and b) not to badmouth the stuff they give you for free and pay you to use.

Other potential future sponsors will also take note of moments like this, so even if you've decided to dump a current sponsor because their stuff keeps breaking, play it cool: No one wants an athlete who word-vomits a bunch of mean stuff about products.

Does that mean you have to fake being happy? Absolutely not. Reporters and photogs want authenticity. So do your sponsors. But remember to be your own spin team: be disappointed, be upset, but don't be angry and don't blame your gear or other people.

There's a difference between explaining and blaming and while it can be a fine line to walk, you need to work on finding it. And post-race, always take the chance to offer a quote. If you don't, there's someone else they can ask, and he or she may not have the best things to say about you—or you'll get left out altogether.

On a happier note, if you have a great race, remember to a) be yourself while b) giving a good soundbite. That means not babbling for five minutes about a single moment in the race (reporters hate transcribing, and video watchers can only listen to you for so long). Try to get as much of your personality to shine through as possible, reference non-race stuff, et cetera—but keep it relatively short.

If a reporter starts glancing around while holding their recorder or video camera, that's a good cue to wrap it up as quickly as possible.

One final tip for dealing with post-race reporters: They're often pretty scattered because there's a lot going on, and they have a ton of people to interview. Try to keep your answers focused and direct, but thoughtful, and don't be afraid to use this as a chance to mention sponsors, past results, upcoming stuff—they're usually not asking super deep questions, so this is your chance to really choose what you want to highlight when the camera is turned on you. (Most reporters will just ask how your race went, and that gives you a ton of options for how to answer!)

Oh—and if you're sweaty/dusty, take three seconds and wipe your face (especially the dirt mustache) and your front teeth. Many a post-race interview has been deemed wildly embarrassing thanks to the combination of a dirt-encrusted upper lip and a chunk of mud between an athlete's front teeth.

Take a moment here to imagine the worst race you've ever had—or if you haven't had one yet, imagine a worst case scenario. Now, imagine that afterwards, you were swarmed by reporters. What are some ways to spin the situation and react positively?

Next task: After your next hard workout, while you're still panting and out of breath and have a skyrocketing heart rate, have your camera ready to go and record a two minute interview talking about your ride like it was a race. This will make you feel like a total dork, but the practice "talking while completely wrecked" will come in handy. Don't wait until after a big race to learn these lessons!

RACE DAY

So... Do Results Matter?

If you don't have results to put on a race resume, no amount of social media attention or baller website setups will get you onto a team. You might get some free swag or a club team invite, but without the actual dedication and results, all the personality in the world might get you a job, but not the racing one that you want.

"I follow cycling very closely. I would not approach an athlete that I hadn't spent time around," says one sponsor. "You cannot make a career out of witty posts without top-level results or being recognized for your work in the team. OK... I can think of two guys that did, but even they were at least qualified to be racing at the level they were at, even if their results didn't show it yet."

So yes—results do matter. And every sponsor, from large to mom-and-pop style, that I interviewed for this agreed that results are a major factor in decisions to hire (and fire) racers. There's always more to the story, but you won't get far without some results to back up your swagger. You might be able to get some ambassador positions, but finding cold, hard cash almost always requires some kind of talent in the sport.

If you don't yet have results but want to make your way onto a team, I would highly recommend doing a few inexpensive local races to establish some kind of baseline for results, and then searching for a club or developmental team in your area. You won't get much by way of $$$$ support, but you'll get experience and later, teams will be happy to know that you already have learned how to work with other people, versus being a lone wolf. Sadly, you won't be making much money for a while—but you probably knew that already.

"At some point, results do matter, to show what an athlete can actually achieve. But to me—and I may be a bit outside the norm—someone who can broadly attract the biggest eyeballs in a way that's becoming of the brands that they represent is also super important," says a CEO of a major athletic clothing brand. "Personality and social reach and metrics are important, but the most critical is finding someone who embodies the personalities and characteristics that are important to the company."

Moral of the story? Start collecting results, because without them, most brands won't notice your personality.

Local races are a great spot to start, and a smart way to work on racing skills and build confidence. Then, focus on slowly moving up to adding in some state or province-level competition, with the eventual goal to get yourself to the bigger races.

Look at your calendar for the upcoming season. What can you rationally expect in terms of results? Not that you should cherry-pick races that will be easy wins, but if you do have some weekends free during a hectic season of high level races, maybe it's time to add a few local ones to the calendar, especially if your current race resume is lacking in podium finishes.

Win Some Races

On the topic of results… As a coach and someone who sees dozens of young racers—and older racers—trying to 'make it' in cycling every year, I've noticed a weird pattern. There are a lot of racers who make the major mistake of not taking wins when they're available.

That might look like:
—Not wanting to race the local series because it's "too easy," despite having a free weekend
—Racing singlespeed instead of racing in the normal Elite category
—"Self-handicapping" by riding to a race and getting there tired
—Immediately upgrading as soon as you technically have enough points, but haven't actually gotten any podiums or wins
—Racing up an age category for 'experience' knowing that a win isn't likely in the higher category, but would be almost certain in their current category

I'm not sure why this is, but I think there are two reasons. The first is actually that the racers are scared of not doing well in a race that they "should easily win." The second is this idea that a race "isn't hard enough for them," so why bother?

No race is too easy once you're racing in the highest category (i.e the Elite field).

No sponsor is going to be impressed by the fact that you didn't race, or that you raced a random category (i.e tandem fat bike instead of elite).

No win isn't worth having. Especially if you're building a race resume.

And lastly, from a training/race tactic perspective, you do need to learn to win. It's a lot different being the person out in front in a race than it is being the person chasing him.

When you're still searching for a team or new sponsors, you can't afford to waste opportunities for wins. They won't come very often once you're in the big races, so take them where you can get them.

Second verse, same as the first: What I said in that last chapter, about looking for a few races to add to your calendar that you think you'll get a solid result in? Do that. I mean it!

Consistency Counts

When you're a young racer, especially one in a sport with age-separated categories, you're going to be racking up plenty of results in the junior field, but do those results matter to a professional team? When you've aged out of the younger categories and into the elite field, team managers and owners value one thing above all else: Consistency.

A singular result, like a national championship or even a world championship, is great... But team owners are really looking for athletes who can consistently produce solid racing results, not just show up for one single day.

Especially as a young athlete, this is going to matter for you: Team owners are trying to extrapolate how you'll do in the pro field, and if they only have one or two good results and a bunch of lackluster performances to go off of, they're less likely to take a bet on you.

So as you're putting together your race resume, or thinking about your season overall, or you're in a race and it isn't going well, remember: It's better to keep all of your results as high as possible versus having a results sheet that reads 30 percent podium finishes, 70 percent DNFs.

Obviously, sometimes DNFs (did not finish) will happen, whether your body or your gear fails you. But don't let a bad race mentally or emotionally keep you from making your way to the finish line. Get through the race—that willingness to suffer, and to make the effort even when things aren't going your way, will matter to a team manager. It shows grit on your part, and that's what they want to see.

Keep Your $hit Tight

If you look around any race weekend and take a moment to assess racers, you'll notice that there are two camps: the riders that always look put together, and the ones that seem to barely make it to the starting line.

That's not because some riders have bigger budgets. Look closely: plenty of those clean-cut riders with perfectly-tuned bikes aren't racing for the big teams... But they might be soon, if they keep that rolling.

Pay particular attention to:

Your Grooming

I'm not going to launch into a 'how you should look' diatribe here, because there isn't one great answer. But there are some basics: clean and tidy. Peter Sagan can get away with ridiculous facial hair. And maybe you can too, if you can toe the line between looking like a crazed serial killer versus a professional with a sense of humor. The difference is in keeping things tidy, not unkempt. The truth is that you're not just a set of legs when a team is bringing you on. They're bringing you on at least in part for your personality and the whole package. Pedaling fast is just a part of the equation, so always be thinking in terms of being team-friendly, even when you're not on one.

On a tight budget: Shower regularly. Don't show up to races already sweaty and smelly. Keep your hair and facial hair under control, whatever that means for you.

Your Kit

Even if you're not on a team, having a clean kit without visible stains, tears or seams coming undone is pro as hell.

On a tight budget: Scout end-of-season sales or go to fallback big-box bike places like Competitive Cyclist or REI, where a simple, unbranded kit is available for under $100. It might not be fancy, but it will look decent. And a stain stick for tough mud spots is money in the bank.

Your Gear
Again, this may not be a team bike, but you can keep your bike dialed and tuned up. AND CLEAN. Don't spend the money on the super pricey set of race wheels, spend it on regular maintenance so that your suspension fork is working and your pedals aren't creaking like crazy. It's not uncommon to spot a bike that clearly cost upwards of five grand pedaling like a Walmart bike because the maintenance isn't there.

On a tight budget: Make friends with the mechanics at a local bike shop, and consider buying an hour of their time to teach you the basics of bike maintenance. And it costs virtually nothing to keep your bike clean: dish soap and WD40 will do the trick. Come to the race venue with a sparkling clean bike. Mechanics—the guys who help choose who gets on a team and who doesn't—notice stuff like that, and are more inclined to help quickly tune your bike if they won't get their hands dirty doing it.

Your Post-Race Getup
I know, I know. You just raced. But when you're done and exhausted, a) don't walk around in your kit, that's gross and will give you saddle sores if you're a cyclist, possibly a UTI as a runner, and b) take a few minutes and clean the salt stains and boogers off of your face. Wash your face, change into clean clothes (without exposing yourself to spectators, please!), and generally try to look put together. I don't mean you need to be wearing Tommy Hilfiger, I just mean you should avoid torn and gross tank tops, sweat-stained shorts, offensive slogans, etc. Take that 10 minutes post-race to clean up, and I can guarantee you'll get better reception.

On a tight budget: Water, towel. Done.

Approaching Race Promoters for Free Entry

First thing to remember: Unless you can prove that your presence at a race will bring in hundreds of amateur riders, YOU ARE NOT DOING THEM A FAVOR BY RACING. You're actually costing them valuable resources, parking spots, et cetera. This notion that because you're racing in the pro category, you deserve to race for free is something that annoys the crap out of most race promoters. Can you score a free entry? Absolutely... But there are right and wrong ways to go about asking for one.

OK, now that that's out of the way, there's nothing wrong with asking for free race entry if you're racing in the elite category. Masters and amateur racers, as a rule, I'm going to recommend not asking for free race entry— it's kind of tacky, unless you're an amateur racer with a hugely successful blog or a masters racer who's willing to volunteer for the entire weekend in exchange for race entry. Basically, only ask if you have value to add to the race. You could, instead, ask for host house recommendations, but when possible, avoid asking flat-out for entries. Promoters do need to earn a living!

And yes, when you're a big-time pro racer with hundreds of thousands of fans, racer organizers will come to you. But unless you're getting emailed constantly with free entry offers, remember these rules when making an ask:

Remember the Email Rules
As previously discussed, address your ask to the right person, make your subject line clear, and keep your email short and sweet.

Be Polite
Again, promoters don't owe you anything. If you start an email with the attitude that you're owed a free entry, you're likely not going to get a response back. Be extremely polite: again, this is a job interview. You're asking to do day labor (or a temp position, in the case of a stage race).

Don't Expect a Promoter to Know Who You Are
Seriously. Promoters get a lot of emails from a lot of people asking for free entry. Back yours up with previous results, and give them a short, succinct argument for why having you at the race will be good for them.

Spell- and Grammar-Check Your Email
Self-explanatory, but often this gets lost in the shuffle. Do a quick read-back and make sure you're making sense. (Sometimes reading an email out loud helps.)

Offer Swag and/or Social Media
Promoters are happiest when you're willing to help out their race in exchange for more than a name on the start list. If you can offer swag, like a signed jersey, as a prize or for a raffle drawing, that can often help your cause. You can also offer to promote the race before and after on your social media (if you promise this, make sure you follow through!).

Offer Time
Ask about opportunities to volunteer your expertise: will there be a 'learn to ride' component where kids can come and be led through the course by pros? Can you be part of an autograph signing? Even if it means losing a couple hours of your day, it's worth it for not just the free entry, but the name recognition and potential new fans you'll develop by showing up for more than just the race.

Trade for Manpower
The easiest way to get free entry is if you can offer a volunteer in exchange. When I was a younger racer trying to make it in the elite field, I would often offer up my dad as a volunteer for the day (a win for him, since it gave him something to do, plus usually some free food and a t-shirt while the race organizer got some added value out of me racing). That worked even when I was starting out! If it's a multi-day event and you don't have a friend or family member to sacrifice, offer your own services. Even offering to stay to help clean up can work. (Note: if you

agree to stay for an event, you are committing to stay for that event. One sponsorship coordinator told me that his biggest turn-off is "reluctantly agreeing to a sponsor visit and then booking a flight out in the middle of it anyway." Yes, that has happened to him. Don't be that guy.)

Say You're Racing Regardless

Don't threaten a promoter that you won't come unless it's a free entry. That's just going to tick them off. Instead, say that you're really excited about the race and will be showing up regardless of the response. (And if you say that, make sure that you mean it—then, when you ask for a free entry next year, the promoter can look back and see that you showed up.)

Don't Get Taken Advantage Of

Like any line of work, there are some people who just aren't great to work with. Some promoters can, to be blunt, be jerks. Some promoters will say you can have free entry, but the task list for getting that entry is worth way more than just paying for the damn race (i.e 3 autograph signings, a ton of social media, several signed jerseys…) Know what your time is worth and consider that before you take the 'free' entry. And if a promoter is rude or dismissive, don't engage or start fighting via email or social media. Tell your team director and email your sport's governing body before starting to troll someone online.

Don't Forget to Register

A secondhand story got back to me during this past race season that illustrates this amazingly well: A group of young racers were brought to a couple of major races. They weren't on the same team, it was a pretty open-ended trip—a development opportunity through their provincial organization. Because of that, it was on the racers to be registered and ready to race. Without going into too much detail, the day before the race, they were picking up numbers and one person wasn't on the registration list.

Why wasn't he on there?

Because he hadn't registered.

Some teams handle your race registration. That's fine. But it never hurts to double check to make sure you're on the list. If you're unsure if the team is going to register you, ask. Most professional races won't let you register within 24 hours of the start, so you really don't want to end up there on race-day just finding out that you're not on that list.

Even with comped entry—actually, especially in cases of comped entry—always check the registration page to make sure your name is on there.

I've seen this happen—and have argued with promoters—quite a bit about this. It's an awkward topic, because you're stoked on free entry and don't want to bug the promoter more than necessary. Unfortunately, I've seen racers who were told that their entries were comped and that they were good to go not make it onto the start list. The promoter who said they'd get comped either forgot he agreed to it, or lied and said he never agreed to free entries.

Hey, like I said, not every promoter is a great person either.

Just double-check your registration. It takes two seconds.

While you're at it, check when your racing license expires. Make a note of that on your calendar as well, since that will also potentially wreck races.

(Pro tip: take a screenshot of your race registration email, and keep a photo of your racing license on your phone as well, so you always have backups.)

A couple months before the season begins, make your race list for the season. Then, while it's still fresh in your mind, find the URLs for race registrations and plug them into your calendar for the day that registration opens (Google Calendar is great here), with a notification turned on so you can't forget. Even if you're not the one doing the race registering, have that list on hand and make sure that if your team manager doesn't send you registration confirmations, you're following up with him or her to make sure you're on the list.

Host Housing and Hospitality

For athletes on a budget, host housing can make or break a season. In fact, let's consider the numbers: if you have a host house in say, Athens, Georgia, for winter training, you're saving potentially thousands of dollars in rent, electricity bills, internet, and maybe even food. That couple thousand dollars can—and should—be looked at as an individual sponsorship. Even weekend stays for races—three or four nights—can save a thousand dollars easily. If you add up the amount you save by staying in host housing compared to hotels, you'll likely be shocked at how much you're actually getting.

With that in mind, be an athlete that people are excited to host. When it comes to host housing, remember the lectures your parents likely gave you before sleepovers when you were a kid. It's easy to keep a host happy, but it's equally easy to offend them. Here are a few tips I've picked up over the years:

Let them know specific plans/needs
Before you arrive, tell your host as many arrival details as you can (ETA, how many bikes you're bringing, departure date, confirmed number of people...). If you have any specific needs or dietary restrictions, tell them ahead of time. It's almost always fine, but I've seen host families get a bit grumpy when they've made a great family-style dinner only to be told that one team member doesn't eat gluten, another doesn't eat meat, et cetera.

Keep your personal space clean and tidy
Even if you have your own room, make sure your personal belongings are tidy, your bed is made and the bathroom stays looking and smelling clean. I've seen host house disasters where toilets were urine-covered, bedrooms

looked like a bomb went off, the kitchen was gross… and the hosts were not impressed. Sure, they shouldn't come into your space, but often, your room is their office or library and they might need access. Just keep it clean. (This is also key for being a good teammate sharing a hotel room.)

Keep your gear immaculate

Always ask where a bike/muddy shoes/surfboard/whatever should be stored, and where it can be washed or cleaned. Don't track dirt or grease in the house, or wreck towels cleaning a chain. (Again, this sounds elementary but I've see it happen!)

Don't abuse the wifi

Ask about if there's an internet limit, and be respectful of it—don't stream HD videos while the family is upstairs trying to watch another movie on Netflix. (Pro tip: hit a public place with wifi, like a coffee shop or a library, and pre-download shows and movies onto your iPad or phone, so you avoid relying on host internet altogether.)

Read the room

Some host families are happy to have you there without making a lot of conversation. Some love the idea of chatting up the pros. Try to get a sense of what your host wants from you in terms of conversation, eating together, etc., and do your best to provide it. Offer to make dinner, or at least offer to wash dishes.

Hook them up

Water bottles are great parting gifts that are always appreciated. Tickets to races that aren't free are also well-received. Even stopping to chat while at the race if your host is there spectating is often much more appreciated than you may realize. And a bottle of wine or a bottle of maple syrup (or some other small token) is a baller move.

Say thanks

In person and in a written note. Again, this is more appreciated than you might realize. If you want to stay with them again the next year, even consider following up with them a few months later to check in, and let them know how your season is going.

Know that they talk about you

For better or worse. I know a lot of hosts, and I've heard them talk a lot of trash about some racers, and have glowingly nice stories about others. Be the one they talk about being great.

So take a moment and practice good behavior now: Send a thank you note or thank you email to someone you've stayed with in the past year (yes, even if that's just mom or dad!). It'll remind you how easy it is to show gratitude and make someone's day.

Training Camp Considerations

Earlier in this book, I mentioned that there are great opportunities for junior level racers if they look at what national or provincial governing bodies are offering for each sport. This is especially true if you're in an Olympic sport, but possible across tons of disciplines.

Once you've applied and gotten accepted, it's time to actually make the most of your training or racing camp. Often, the coaches at these camps are coaches with other teams, working as team managers, or will be asked by teams for their opinions on specific riders.

With that in mind:

—Be polite. Seriously, please and thank you go a long way towards impressing the coaches on these camps.

—Show up prepared. Have working and clean gear, broken-in shoes, whatever stuff is required for your sport. Have your drink mix, ride or run food. If we're talking cycling, bring a ton of flat-fixing gear. Cross-country running? Extra spikes and shoe laces. Come with more than you think you'll need, and have spare everything.

—Keep your stuff clean throughout. Don't let your suitcase explode, even in your own room. Coaches notice this and they don't appreciate it. If your gear gets dirty, be the first to get to the hose after a ride.

—Keep yourself clean throughout. No one likes the smelly, sweaty kid at dinner, and frankly, it's unsanitary. I've seen a few riders get uninvited from future camps because of bad hygiene.

—Change and shower after rides/runs. One of my (and a lot of other coaches') major pet peeves is athletes who hang out in their sweaty, gross cycling or running gear for hours after a workout, walking around the kitchen, sitting on the couch, getting sweat and whatever else everywhere. Even if you can't get in the shower right away, change after the workout.

—Bring GasX and/or Pepto Bismol. This one is gross and hard for me to even write about, but the gas levels among junior and U23 boys are ridiculous. It is NOT a point of pride to be stinking up the house, especially during dinner. This might sound silly if you're new to the training camp environment, but I know some guys who haven't gotten on teams because they just smelled too terrible to be around. So if you know you get gassy on big ride days, bring something like GasX to calm that down. (If this is you, consider working with a nutritionist to calm your stomach down!)

—Ask for advice. Coaches are there to help you and want to help you—so whatever you're wondering about, ask the coaches. (This also impresses us, because it shows you actually care about the camp and developing in the sport.)

—Seriously, get a coach to check your rider resume/website/social media and offer tips while you're there. Again, great way to connect with a coach and get some valuable tips.

—Follow the rules. I know a few great athletes who are no longer invited to camps because they snuck out at night, or acted like asshats during rides, or, in one memorable case, egged another athlete's house.

—Be a leader—not a dictator. Offer to lead cooking team dinner or a meal one night, or try to be helpful to other riders getting their stuff ready in the morning (once your own gear is taken care of). Coaches notice who's naturally becoming the leader of the group, but they also notice who's just bossing everyone around. Guess who they like more?

—Don't do dumb $hit. Your goal is to be able to do every day's workout, or do your best in the race. Know the point of the camp, and work accordingly. Don't do an extra run or hike at the end of a long ride if you know you have another hard ride tomorrow. People aren't impressed by someone who does extra work if it means they can't perform the next day.

Really, a camp like this is just a lead up to what will hopefully be a full life of team camps and trips to fun locations, so make the most of it.

A Note on Spending $ $ $

Once you turn competitive in any sport, it gets expensive. But sometimes, you have to spend money to make money. As with being a jerk in host housing, word gets around if you're the cheapskate on a team, the one who insists on not paying part of the cleaning fee at an AirBNB because you 'didn't make a mess,' or the guy who reminds a teammate for months that he owes you a dollar (granted, the guy should pay you back. But still!).

I know you're probably not making much (any) money, if you're reading this. And I'm not saying you have to start buying rounds of drinks or pick up the dinner tab when you're out with fellow cyclists. But don't be stingy and skimp on the tip when splitting the bill either. Don't go into debt, but if you end up spending an extra $20 a month to not be 'that guy,' it's money well-spent, and it will come back to you in other ways later.

If you really can't afford something, the answer is simple: don't do it.

There are countless examples of riders (who I won't throw under the bus in this book) who have gotten "not invited to return" to a team because during the year, all they did was nickel and dime management (usually while complaining about the team). Managers and team directors want to help you, but if all they hear from you is "Will you cover this?" or "I need more money," it's a turnoff.

Think really hard before you hit anyone up for cash. Pause before making any money asks, and think really hard about what your life has looked like lately. Have you gone on expensive trips, or posted on social media about any major buys? I know one guy who was constantly asking for support from the national team, but if you checked his social media, he was also spending a ton of time traveling to train in sunny spots in Europe, and posting photos of massive meals out with friends. If you're going to angle for needing money for travel that normally wouldn't get covered or that you don't qualify for, it's probably wise to make sure your social media isn't showing off all your $hit, James-Franco-in-Springbreakers-style.

You can be frugal without being a jerk about it. If teammates are going to a pricey dinner, there's a way to politely decline—or go, but make sure you're not ordering drinks and then complaining about splitting the bill.

Side note: ALWAYS have enough to cover tax and tip as well as your food when eating out. (I see young athletes guilty of this all the time.) This is a weirdly big issue since it's culturally sensitive. In Europe, you don't have to tip as much, though leaving a bit is polite. In Canada, tip, but think 15 percent. In the US, 18 to 20 percent is more the norm. If you're not sure what the expectation is, do a quick Google search. Try to be reasonable about tipping, and take that and tax into account when putting in your share for dinner. Everyone hates the guy who calculates what he owes for food but neglects tax/tip.

Lastly—if you owe money, pay it ASAP. Nothing makes teammates/managers/friends less inclined to hook you up again than if they have to chase you down for a rent check, race entry fee, or money from the last three dinners.

Pause and think about any money you might still owe people. Then, pay it back. If you're in an offseason or have some spare time, think about ways to pocket some extra cash now for when you need it later, maybe by selling some old gear.

In- and Post-Race Notes

If you're reading this, I hope this is self-explanatory. But like many of the other points in this book that I initially thought were obvious… I was still seeing people ignore basic rules of decency over and over again, so this advice is worth sharing. Let's emphasize just how important good sportsmanship is, regardless of how talented you are as a racer.

For his biggest athlete turn-offs, a major bike brand's sponsorship coordinator lists: "Quitting a race in an attention-seeking way and disrespecting the other racers and promoter."

In the heat of the moment, especially if a race doesn't go the way you hoped or if another athlete pushes into you or causes you to crash, it can be tempting to throw your bike or throw a punch. Don't do it.

(In fact, one team doctor told me that the dumbest yet most common injuries he sees post-race in road riders is various bruised/broken/swollen hands from punching something harder than bone post-race… Especially bad news for cyclists, who aren't known for having the strongest bones or the straightest punches.)

Deep breathes, cool head.

Sponsors—and potential sponsors—would rather see a rider who can handle adversity or a bad situation with a smile, or at the very least, without a temper tantrum. The best riders, and the ones with the best contracts, are the ones who can still smile and shake hands with people in the crowd (and save the argument with other racers for when no one else is watching).

You don't need to be a Zen master, but you do need to be a professional. Again, imagine you're working in an office, not on a race course. If a fellow employee stole your idea, or cut you off mid-sentence, you wouldn't throw a punch or curse him out. You might talk to your boss later (and you should report offenses to race officials after the stage or race is over). But you wouldn't really get crazy in the middle of a presentation unless you were OK with being escorted out by security.

Even great racers will get kicked off teams if their tempers are too hard to handle.

Post-race, if things didn't go your way, try to find somewhere private to sulk—offer short sound-bites to interviewers explaining what happened, but don't start ranting about the event or other racers, even if that's how you feel. Try to maintain a high degree of chill until you're alone or with trusted friends before having a freak out. Promoters, team directors and other racers will all be more impressed by your grace under pressure than they will about a temper tantrum that you're throwing—and, to be honest, a tantrum never got anyone a better score.

If you do believe there's a reason to dispute results, for example, if another rider actually shoved you or hit you, then quietly go speak to a race official about it as soon as possible, before results are made official. There's nothing wrong with contesting results, the key is in how you approach the official. Don't forget, he or she wasn't the one who wrecked your race, and taking it out on the official will absolutely not help your case.

So take a few minutes here and think about a few of your past races. Even if you didn't throw a punch, list a couple of the ways that you could have been a better sport at the finish. Whether that means taking a minute to high five a few fellow competitors, chatting with some younger kids who are excited to be around fast guys and girls, or even just thanking the promoter (or the race officials). Now that you have that list, try to remember it at the end of your next race. You'll develop a much better reputation.

Always Be Nice & Friendly (Sincerely) at Races

A quick story to illustrate this lesson. One racer, Dave, was crushing a MTB race on the weekend. He was absolutely tearing up the field. Behind him—a few minutes behind—in seventh, was another racer, Jason. (I am making these names up to protect the innocent, and the guilty.)

Jason had chatted with the announcer earlier in the day about racing and how the announcer was doing with a nagging injury, and he helped out at a kids 'learn to ride' clinic that morning. Despite doing terribly (for him) in the race, the announcer spent more time talking about Jason ("He told me he has a cold, but he is racing like an animal!") throughout the painful laps. About Dave, he pretty much just announced his name and position—even though he was in third.

Guess which sponsor was happier at the end?

Second story: I was recently going on a run as the pros were warming up at a race. All but one of the pros who passed me smiled, waved, nodded or said hi, even the ones who didn't know me. Except one, who did know me but looked right at me—and right through me—and just glared.

Next article I have to write where I need pro opinions, I won't go to him. If I was sponsoring a team, I wouldn't hire him. If I was a team manager, I wouldn't recommend him.

First point: That person you're rude to or ignoring? He or she just might make or break your career. (And as a writer and former sponsor/team manager, I can tell you I didn't hire that guy, and haven't interviewed him since then. And remember… Word gets around.)

Second point: Even if I was just out for a run, completely unrelated to the race, and happened to pass you, being polite costs you nothing, while being actively rude is a surefire way to make people dislike cyclists in general… And it's bad karma for you anyway.

Third point: It is SO damn easy to be reasonably friendly. I promise, it won't kill you. And it will get you everywhere. "If you wake up and choose that niceness is going to be your default, you feel better about what you're doing," one longtime pro racer told me.

Sure, winning is great—but being nice to people (truly nice, not just pretend nice) will 10x your value to sponsors and make you a much more attractive prospect.

But it's not always the easiest thing to do if you're not in the habit.

You can start doing this right now. Every day this week, give one person a compliment—a real one. Mix it up and do this on the phone, over email and in-person. If it feels natural, great—you're crushing it. But if it's not something that feels comfortable, that just means you need to practice that particular skill a little bit more.

SOCIAL MEDIA

Making Nano-Influencer Status Work for You

Recently, terms like micro-influencer and nano-influencer have been tossed around to describe people with small but loyal followings. So if you don't have 50K followers, you can still use your audience to help you secure sponsors, but it won't look the same as that 1.5 million follower athlete/influencer. For example, if you're more of a community-level racer, you're going to want to tailor your content to be more community-centered versus trying for global/big-name appeal—at least part of the time.

In fact, you have a leg-up over the more traditional influencers with huge followings. Research has shown influencer engagement is dropping because people are sick of being sold to by influencers with 5 million followers, and the analytics firm InfluencerDB has said that influencers with under 10,000 followers are actually a better investment because they have higher engagement despite smaller reach.

So how can you make this work for you, especially at home?

Support Local Biz
Even before you can reach out for partnerships, make your local spaces shine on your social accounts. Don't just post close-up selfies from your recent run, post pictures of the trailhead and give intel on where it is and how the trails are, for example. This way, you're helping create a local buzz.

Get Involved In Your Community
Join a club or two if you're not already involved in local events, and do small collabs with local brands and clubs—even a small following means something to them, if most of your followers are local!

Work With Small Community-Based Brands

Think more local when it comes to approaching sponsors on the basis of your social media accounts if you're in the nano-numbers versus a six-figure following. A local yoga studio is more likely to want to work with you as a yogi doing cool poses in and around town and plugging them versus a huge company like Gaiam that boasts millions of followers already.

Still Think Big

This isn't to say every post needs to be #shoplocal. You can still keep your normal content rolling—and you should, because as you do grow as an influencer/athlete, you may want to be able to move up in the influencer space, working with bigger and more globally oriented brands.

Approaching Social Media: The Do's

2 Here

"These days, social media is vital. I keep hearing professionals lamenting that less-talented riders with better SM presence are getting better contracts," says one sponsor. It's annoying, if you're not into social media, but it's a fact of life at this point. Even if you're not a fan of Instagram or Twitter, make your social media work for you.

Be psyched on bikes (or whatever sport you're in).
You have an awesome profession (or semi-profession), and you should be psyched on it! Photos of you and your bike, your bike, your cycling friends... Just let people know how much you dig on bikes/running/whatever your sport is. "Try to at least act like you care," says one marketing director. Simple... Kind of. How do you do that without being obnoxious?

Be consistent
Try to post relatively consistently: That doesn't mean every day, it just means not posting 20 pictures one day, then nothing for three months. Find what works for you and feels comfortable: For most pro athletes, that's posting 4-5 times per week, but interacting on a daily basis to respond to comments or put a Story on Instagram versus a Post.

Post action shots
People engage more when there's action, and sponsors like this because it's a subtle way of promoting their gear (i.e a photo of you hitting a corner, and a few words about how the tires have great hook-up, versus just a photo of a box of tires).

Be Informative
Think about skills you've learned over the years and how those could help other athletes. This is the kind of information people love. Videos on really

specific tips and tricks are great. For a cyclist, this could look like mounting tires with a tip about how to get a tire on the rim without tire levers. For a runner, this could look like a tip on how to avoid a hydration pack bouncing. Share a tip every once in a while and your audience will feel like there's more value to following you.

Don't be afraid to be goofy.
People love athletes with personality, not just ones with a lot of speed. Be your oddball self! Not every post has to be strictly about sport. (A lot of athletes make the mistake of not sharing their lives, just their racing, when most fans would love some behind-the-scenes info.)

Post photos sponsors/media can use.
You may get some great shots from photographers to post with the proper credit, but make sure your feed isn't 100 percent photographer-shot. A few decent photos—even a well-framed selfie—that a sponsor or media person can grab for their own use makes you a lot more likely to get featured on other sites/in the media. (Story-time: At one magazine, I was putting together a piece on the 10 cyclists you have to follow on Instagram, and I had to nix quite a few who had great feeds because they didn't have any images that weren't taken by a pro photographer. Since photogs can get grumpy when their work is used in a magazine without permission, I had to scratch those racers from the list.)

Share real information.
Fans and followers love getting 'insider info' about how you're gluing tires in a special way, or what tire pressure you're running for a race, or how to be more comfortable on a descent. Share what scares you, share what's making you excited about your sport.

Spell check.
(You might be sensing a theme here.)

Encourage participation.
Ask questions, use fun hashtags, take part in cool social media initiatives from the companies that sponsor you—engage your audience. But if you engage your audience, make sure you also engage back with them!

Keep your community positive
Respond when you can, but positively. You might not be able to respond to

everything if you have too many interactions (a good problem), but try to like/favorite/heart/whatever positive messages, respond to questions, and say thank you to fans.

Take advantage of platform features.
Instagram now has Stories, slideshows, videos—and a million other add-ons. If you have the time, play around and have fun trying new parts of social media. Don't let yourself fall into the trap of getting stale with your posts and the style of social media that you are using.

Always Be Authentic.
The best thing you can do for your social media is to put your true self out there—don't try to copy another athlete's style or feed. Just be you.

Approaching Social Media: The Don'ts

2 here

Rule number one: assume that your sponsors are always looking at your social media. Whether you Instagram, Tweet, Snapchat or Facebook (or whatever other site you're using), know that it's no longer something just your friends are looking at. If you want to be a professional athlete, remember: You're a professional athlete now. So, avoid these entirely-too-common missteps:

Do not: stress about followers/likes.
Organic growth is slow—so don't worry if your numbers aren't as high as other pros. Freaking out leads to dumb mistakes like buying followers (sponsors do not love this!), or hashtagging insane amounts to artificially inflate your Likes. Keep it simple and authentic.

Do not: post "Look at all my $hit photos."
You know the ones: "Christmas came early" captioned under a pile of boxes delivered to your doorstep. Sponsor-correct photos talking about loving a certain product are great, but no one *really* cares if a bike box showed up at your house. You're just bragging. And virtually every sponsor I chatted with says that posts like that, especially when the item is still in the box, do absolutely nothing for the brand and only serve to remind followers that athletes are getting stuff for free and obviously will be talking about how great it is.

Do not: Simply unbox.
"Professionals I have worked with know my biggest pet peeve: box photos—doorstep and otherwise," says one sponsorship coordinator. "It's amateur to take a snap of four bike boxes with UPS labels on your doorstep. Your fans don't want to see it and it commodifies the brand. Unpacking and making a little display of the energy bars or eyewear that you just took

delivery of is just obnoxious." However, there is a way to do this tactfully. Instead of just showing the UPS boxes of your bikes at your curb, what about doing a time elapsed video of you unboxing them and putting them together? Can you add some service-oriented tip to your unboxing experience so that the viewer gets something out of it? Think about ways to make creative, fun content around unboxing if you want to do it, or if your sponsors ask you to.

Do not: curse excessively.
Once in a while, if that's your thing, go for it: you won't lose your following for dropping the occasional swear word. But do consider your audience, and consider this: the most popular endurance athletes on social media keep it clean. If you're trying to appeal to or represent a family-friendly brand, be particularly mindful of that. (Look at the language that your sponsors or dream sponsors tend to use if you need some reference points.)

Do not: go negative, all the time.
(And apologies for that double negative.) Authenticity is great, and if you have a bad day or a bad season, you shouldn't feel the need to pretend everything is fine. But by the same token, no one really wants to read post after post about how rough you have it. Look for the fun moments and share those as well—and doing this might even change your outlook on the season!

Do not: complain about your gear.
A sponsor's worst nightmare is to wake up to a post from an athlete slamming the bike/shoes/sunglasses/etc. that he was given. If you have a problem with the product, go to the company first—don't let them know via social media. "Don't shit on the brand. We shouldn't have to tell you to not post or show things that aren't in line with the sponsor—complaints, blatantly using other brands… that stuff," says one sponsorship coordinator. Should be obvious, sometimes isn't.

Do not: post only selfies, all the time.
Selfies aren't inherently bad. When every picture is a selfie, however, that gets a little old. Change it up.

Do not: post anything you wouldn't want your grandmother to see.
This can vary from person to person, and there's no hard and fast rule for

what's too risqué to post and what isn't: depends on what message you're trying to send and what you're comfortable with. So, to put this minefield of a topic simply, post what you want, but make sure that you're OK with everyone—from a younger brother to a high school ex to a new sponsor to a team director—seeing the photo today, and in five years.

Do not: post tons of 'holding gear' photos.
I'll say it again: People like to see gear in action, and while the occasional "I love this jersey" post is fine, make sure you're including plenty of movement-focused photos.

Do not: overuse hashtags.
Anything over five, don't include in the original post. If you want to use more, add a comment with all of the extra ones.

Do not: engage with trolls.
When people are actively trying to goad you into a fight, don't take the bait. A rational discussion is a different story, but don't waste your time in pointless battles. "I've seen riders use social in ways that aren't becoming for themselves or their sponsors. Stay away from pissing matches or off-color comments," adds one major brand's marketing director. (One pro racer I know will direct argumentative people to her contact page on her website and say that she'll have a discussion over email, not on a public forum, and often that shuts things down… and most trolls don't bother emailing.)

Stay in Your Lane (Mostly)

Video is huge right now. Podcasts are taking off. But you're more of a writer than a videographer. Should you go to video? Maybe.

The thing is, if you're going to do video, you can't be half-assed about it. That's why plenty of influencers and athletes stay away from it, though plenty have made moves to embrace it.

If you are interested in learning a new media, that's awesome—there are great resources like Skillshare for courses, or even just YouTube or a million other free resources to help you. But if you're not willing to put the time or effort into learning the new platform, just stay on the ones that you use and enjoy the most.

I've seen hundreds of pro athletes post one or two awkward videos on YouTube before turning back to Instagram, and while it's fine to test the waters, you're likely better off focusing on the platforms that you enjoy and find easy and fun to use, not the ones that are clunky and hard-to-manage for you.

The only exception is that while having a large following on any one channel is great, the odds are good that that channel won't exist in the same form in a few years. (Anyone remember MySpace?) So while you should stick with the platforms you like, make sure your basic website is maintained and up to date, at the least. And don't be afraid to try new platforms—just remember that they don't always have to be for you.

Social Media: The Weird Questions

Social media is changing every year, and more recently, a trend I've seen with young athletes (and young people in general) is the use of a "finsta" (a 'fake instagram' or secondary account on any channel).

I don't want to sound like an old fogey writing this, but I do want to address it briefly. Having a secondary channel for yourself as an athlete when you aren't famous is honestly kind of weird—especially if your 'secret' social media channel is still open and searchable under your name!

Case in point: There's a young guy who races in the US who runs two Instagrams. On his 'athlete' page, he has under 100 followers and the posts are generically appropriate (and kind of boring). Then, his second page— that pops up before his athlete page when you search his name!—is filled with cursing, photos of boozing it up at parties (despite being underage) and it's generally a little scandalous.

If you want to have that secondary page to show off partying photos to your friends, I'm not going to stop you. (I will, however, caution you to not be a dumbass about it, and think about how you'd feel if your parents did find that page.)

But I'm also going to point out that it's just idiotic to have two separate, completely opposite accounts that are SEARCHABLE AND OPEN. Guys, be smart about this. If you want to have that private account, set it to private, and don't use your actual name. (And make sure your profile picture is reasonably respectable in the event someone stumbles on the page, since the tiny profile pic is still public.)

If a sponsor finds the picture of your 16-year-old self shotgunning a beer with your pants down, he's not going to care that you didn't post it to your athlete page, just to your personal page. It's still out there on the internet, and fans can find it. Anything and everything that gets onto the internet can be made public—with or without your consent.

Look at some of the biggest names in the sport: I can almost guarantee 99 percent of those athletes are using one singular page, not running a double life. And since you don't have a ton of time to waste on social media anyway, it doesn't really make sense to waste that time on a page that people aren't supposed to see. If you want to be taken seriously, this isn't the way to do it.

And lastly, the whole secret account page unfortunately tends to pull a lot of your focus from your actual athlete social media account, which is the one you should be building and working on.

PS: Also understand that no amount of hiding your account will guarantee that it's hidden. But I highly recommend that if you insist on having the private account separate from your athlete one, and if there's anything on there that you don't want sponsors to see, a) make it private and b) don't use your name.

A Word on Social Media Sexiness

One topic that comes up time and time again in both the athletic sphere and the influencer world, especially for women, is this idea of 'is it OK to be sexy?' (And followed by that... What are we defining as sexy?)

This is a difficult topic, but please understand that I'm not talking about the ethics or morality here—I'm talking strictly about the economics and thinking critically about this in the context of your career. And for some, this may be a surprise, but 'sexy' doesn't always win the economic debate, especially in the fitness industry!

There isn't a right or wrong answer, but there is this warning: You need to be deliberate in what you do. If you're comfortable posting bikini shots on the regular, that's great—but be aware that some people are going to complain about it. You might have certain brands that want to work with you more the sexier your social feed is, but you may also lose certain brands.

Do what feels right for you, but understand what doing it means.

If you are searching for sponsors or advertisers, consider checking out other athletes and influencers who work with those brands. You'll get a sense of what types of people that sponsors tend to go for, and you can make an informed decision about how to your posts will be received.

You also want to consider who you want as your audience. There are plenty of fitness influencers, like Kayla Itsines, who manage to rock the hell out of a sports bra without going into over-the-top sexy photoshoot territory. There are women like the founders of Tone It Up who crush it in bikinis and still appeal to a female demographic... But there are also a lot of fitness 'influencers' who opt for uber-sexy accounts that end up with a large following, which might boost your number of likes… but it won't necessarily convert to clicks or sales for a brand.

And if you're hoping to attract ad dollars, if you have zero conversion from pic to click, you won't keep an advertiser on board for long. Your audience needs to look similar to the audience of your sponsors, advertisers or team for it to be useful to a company.

I'm 100 percent in favor of your right to choose how you wants to appear on social media. But you have to understand that your choice matters.

One last word of advice: If you're a minor, be even more thoughtful here. Sponsors and advertisers will almost never sponsor/promote a minor who posts tons of super-sexualized images on his or her feed, simply because there are some legal/ethical risks involved there for the sponsor.

In the last few years, I've gotten to work with a bunch of amazing young women on a whole host of different projects. Most of the time, linking to their Instagrams in articles was no big deal. But I ran into a couple where I couldn't actually link to any of their stuff: The girls were amazing, fantastic teenagers with a ton going for them. But their profiles were so over-the-top sexualized that I couldn't link to them in posts that were meant for a young readership—or any readership, really, considering these young women were minors. The result? The interviews were great, but the interviewees didn't get much benefit: No new followers, no new sponsors.

So if your grandmother wouldn't approve it and you're under 18, probably avoid posting.

A Social Scheduling Tip

I'm the first to admit that making sure all of your social media obligations get met, and met well, is a freaking full time job sometimes. But sponsors don't take "I don't have time" or "I didn't have a good photo" as a great excuse. Authenticity is fantastic and all of your scheduled posts should still be 100 percent true to you, but that doesn't mean they can't be decent quality and well-timed. So, let's talk about the practicalities of making your social feeds solid.

Enlist a friend for a photoshoot
This could be a teammate, a parent, a partner, a buddy, the old guy next door that sits on his porch all day—you don't need a professional photographer to get some good shots of you on the bike or on a run. Once a month, try to take a series of photos, showcasing (tastefully) new gear plus some sweet skills. Doing this means you'll never be at a loss for photos when a sponsor asks for one, or when it's time to post. Speaking of time to post...

Set a schedule
If you're still in school, consider social media for sponsors like a homework assignment. If you're working, consider it a work project. Regardless of what you're doing, make sure it's in your calendar. When a sponsor asks for one social media post a week, make sure you have a note weekly to put up a photo. If a sponsor just asks that you mention them in social media, around once a week is probably appropriate. And again, don't feel like every post needs to be a huge, blatant ad for your sponsor. Having your sports drink hover in the background behind the water bottles you're filling is perfect—just make sure you tag them so they know about it!

Batch 'em
Normal social media shouldn't cease to exist for you, but you can save a ton of stress and last minute freakouts by taking 30 minutes once a week

to schedule the more sponsor-correct, properly labeled and hashtagged posts, and then post your normal fun stuff throughout. Apps like Hootesuite and Buffer are free/cheap and make life a lot easier. (Instagram can be tricky to schedule but both of those apps have workarounds.) Even storing a few things in Twitter and Instagram Drafts can simplify your week.

Before you start downloading apps (that you'll quickly forget unless you go into them with a plan), take a moment to list out your current social media obligations to sponsors, and draft a quick look at what a week should look like (including appropriate hashtags that sponsors have asked you to use and @ mentions).

It could look something like this, splitting a table into a rough weekly schedule. You'll change it over time, but this gives you a good blueprint so you won't hit Saturday every week and need to do 25 tweets back-to-back to meet requirements. Note that there's also a column for normal content too. You'll also have your more spontaneous posts, but having a plan for at least one un-sponsored tweet/gram/snap per day makes sure that you're not creating a completely advertorial feed:

	CONTENT	BIKE COMPANY A	SUNGLASSES COMPANY B	CLOTHING COMPANY C
MON	Ride	@BikeCompanyA #roadslikethese	@SunglassesCoB #myshades	---
TUES	Run	---	---	@ClothingCoC
WED	Link	@BikeCompanyA #whyweride	---	---
THURS	Blog	---	@SunglassesCoB #sunnyday	@ClothingCoC #cyclingkit

Your schedule might not look like this, you might post much more or less frequently. It's not about mimicking this exactly with daily obligations, just making sure you're hitting your required targets!

Hosting a DIY Photoshoot

If you can't find a photographer willing to shoot you for no $$$, find a few friends in the same boat and host a photoshoot day. A friend, teammate or parent is usually willing to help you out with this.

Alternatively, if you're flying totally solo, use the video trick to avoid selfies and get some rad action shots. Simply set up your camera to video mode (in the best resolution possible) and film yourself for a few minutes. Take a few runs towards the camera each time, so you definitely capture something worth using. But rather than posting the video, grab screenshots so you have still images. It's not the best option, but works in a pinch!

I don't love doing these shoots—they feel super awkward—but they make life a lot easier when it comes to writing blog posts and social media posts, and for providing good, quality (flattering) photos to sponsors. This ended up being one of the longest chapters I wrote because the right photos can make a major difference in how a potential sponsor perceives you.

My recommendations when running one of these photoshoot days:

Find the Right Person
Teammates can be the best and the worst choices for photographer-for-a-day, so pick wisely. If you're planning on shooting photos of each other, set specific time limits so one of you doesn't hog the spotlight. (Seriously, use the timer on your phone.) If you're enlisting a friend, make sure it's someone you feel comfortable with, because getting your photo taken can feel really uncomfortable.

Make It Count
Use multiple kits, find a spot that has a few locations (I usually try to do

either riding/running on the same trail, or find a trail near a road so I can mountain bike and road bike), and prep your props (food, water bottles, all the little stuff from sponsors that rarely makes it into racing photos) so you're not on the side of the trail wasting time getting ready.

...Or Use Races
Post-race, grab a teammate and get some photos done while you're still in recovery mode. The photos will be super authentic, and it's an easy time since all your gear is in one place and ready to go!

See What Other Sponsored Riders Are Doing
Check what other riders sponsored by the same company as you are doing in their photos, especially photos that get re-shared by the companies. Don't copy them, but use them as a great source of inspiration.

Create a "Shot List"
When you're heading out to do this shoot, take a few minutes to list what images you're hoping to get out of it. It can be as simple as shots on an up-hill, shots going around a corner, shots holding the bike over your head... Or it can be as specific as "shot of me eating a protein bar while lying on the ground next to the trailhead, looking tired." Also list the specific gear that you're trying to get in the shot (i.e different food/clothing/etc. for different sponsors). The more prepared you are, the less likely that you'll forget that you wanted that dousing-your-face-with-the-water-bottle picture.

Shoot the Gear
On that note, this is a good time to get some decent non-unboxing style shots of your gear. Lean your bike up against a graffiti-covered wall, shoot your muddy sneakers drying on a rock, get creative! At least this way, your photos aren't generic product shots.

A Side Note About Products
Remember, if you're hoping to get re-grammed, re-shared or posted on a sponsor's website, they don't want competitors in the photo. So, if you have a drink sponsor and a food sponsor, try to get some shots where the drink isn't in sight and it's just about the food. If you have a clothing sponsor but a cycling cap or gloves from another company, get a few shots where you're not wearing the cap.

Get Moving

The photos of you actually riding or running versus standing with your bike or posed on the trail will do a lot better for you and be more likely to get picked up by sponsors. Pro tip: try to act as natural as possible but go in slow motion so your photos don't end up blurry.

Get a Crew Together

Shots with multiple people do really well, especially if you're both sponsored by the same company, so when possible, grab a friend!

Don't Overdo

Try to look as natural as possible. A slightly dirty bike is totally fine in an action shot. A look of concentration is great. Just be as natural and authentic as possible. (But make sure you're happy with how you look so the photos don't end up tossed because you had mud in your teeth!)

Get Psyched on Bloopers

Don't delete your blooper reel—if you ended up with some mud-in-teeth shots, keep them. They may end up being the funniest and cutest of the bunch, or at least will lead to some fun behind-the-scenes Instagram Story content.

Mix It Up

While a look of concentration is great, try a few smiling shots. Do different tricks, ask your friend to shoot at different angles, try funny stuff! (I also find that the best shots are the ones where you're not looking at the camera, so take a few where you're talking to/looking at someone 'off camera')

Do a Lot with a Little

Take advantage of the time that you have, and shoot in multiple outfits with different backgrounds. That way, you have content for weeks without anyone suspecting it was all shot on the same day.

Bring a Changing Skirt

(Or a big beach towel.) This makes for much less scandalous costume-changes if you have a few pairs of shorts/tights you want to shoot in.

Check the Film While On Location

The dumbest mistake I've made in these shoots is assuming my photographer friend captured the exact images that I was hoping for... Only to come home and find that in almost every picture, I was blurred beyond recognition, had a contorted look on my face, or was just shot at the least flattering angle ever. You don't need to check every single shot or drive your friendly photographer insane, but just ask to look at what they've taken a couple times during the shoot and save yourself the re-shoot.

Use Sport Mode on a Camera

Serious influencers tend to use real cameras to shoot most of their images so that the quality is high. If you have access to a decent digital camera and you're taking action shots, unless you're a great photographer, stick it in sport mode. The quality won't be amazing but the photos also won't be blurry. (Most cameras and smartphones also have continuous shoot mode, so it takes a ton of pictures when you depress the button—that's great for action shots.)

...And Play with Video on Your Phone

If you're having trouble with blurry action shots because you're stuck with just a phone camera, you can still get decent (small) images by shooting a video of the action in the highest resolution possible, then screen-shotting frames from the video. I usually ask a photographer to do this a few times during a shoot to guarantee something useable.

Be Shadow-Aware

Again, you'll catch this if you check the film before heading home, but try to find a location that's either not shadowed or entirely shady. A lot of shadows mean that unless you're an absolute pro photographer, the images will likely suck.

Magic Hour

Right ahead of dusk—around 4PM—is the photographer's golden hour, where the lighting is ideal to avoid shadows and give you a good glow. Try to time your shoot for then!

Shoot a Lot More Than You Think You Need

You will end up hating a lot of pictures, to be honest. Especially if you've enlisted the help of someone who isn't a professional or has no photo experience, so tell him or her to just. keep. shooting. (I'm a huge fan of candids, and I think they look the best, so ask him or her to shoot even when you're not specifically posing for pictures. You get great shots like that!)

Don't Be Afraid to Give Direction
My worst shoots come when I'm feeling nervous with whoever I've enlisted to help me out and I'm not giving them any direction, just relying on them to shoot. Especially when dealing with a non-photography-loving buddy, you're going to want to offer ideas and advice, and suggest spots to shoot and different angles. He or she will be happier to have advice and get the right shot than have you unhappy with the photos at the end of the day.

Try to Be Unexpected
Do fun, goofy, cool stuff that isn't the same old running/riding/jumping shots. If you're trail running, get a shot of you climbing a tree, or playing in the stream by the trail—try a few things out, and you might come up with some amazing shots.

Thank Your Photographer
Even if your dad is the guy you enlisted to help you out, make sure you say thanks and buy him dinner or at least a coffee. The guy is taking two hours or more out of his life to help you out, so the least you can do is say thanks!

Have Fun
The easiest way a photoshoot can go downhill is if you're stiff and awkward and uncomfortable with the idea that someone is taking your picture. It can feel a little silly to ask someone to take a ton of pictures of you, and it's easy to get self-conscious. Just try to remember that your friend doesn't think you're a dork, he is psyched to help you—that's why he agreed to come along.

Creating an Athlete Website

You don't need to be an internet genius or design an amazing site, but if you're going to be a serious athlete, it's helpful to have a simple site set up with your basic information, some key results and photos, and contact information.

Sure, you can do this with a Facebook page as well—but for old-school reporters and sponsors, it's nice to have a simple landing page with relevant information, and the more old-fashioned team managers and owners appreciate being able to see basic information at a glance without navigating Facebook.

Should you blog on your website? A lot of racers think setting up a site means blogging, but that's absolutely not the case. To blog or not to blog is entirely up to you: a website doesn't have to include a journal, though that can be a great way of interacting with fans. But if you don't think you have a lot to say, or don't enjoy writing, don't worry about that. Just make a basic page with stats, sponsors, contact info and links to your social media.

Use a simple, free platform like Wordpress or Wix and choose a basic template. (Wordpress has gone from being just a blogging platform to a great web development tool.) You can add sidebars with your Twitter and Instagram feeds to make the page seem less static, and choose a fun, dynamic picture of you to feature.

Willing to spend a couple bucks? The premium version of Wordpress isn't free, but allows you to personalize the URL, which is much more pro. (It also gets rid of some ads and gives you an @YOURNAME.com email.)

A note on themes: What was in style five years ago might look super dated now. (This is a problem my own sites, and every magazine I've ever worked with, has contended with, so you're not alone.) So don't be afraid to change things up and give your site a fresh new theme. Even the "expensive" ones on Wordpress are usually under $50, so if you find a template you love (the site allows you to preview how your content would look on different themes), it's money well spent.

Another mistake is not having contact info on there, which happens more often than you'd think! The main reason you're using this page is so people can reach you—so make sure they have a way to reach you. You can use an actual contact form on the site (make sure you check where responses are forwarded to), or just list your email (don't put your email in full, do something like molly [at] gmail [dot] com to help avoid spam and robots snagging your email).

As someone who's constantly searching for athletes to interview for various articles, I can't stress enough how much greater your chances of getting featured in a magazine or on a website are if you just have your contact information available. Especially when searching for athletes for pieces like "best warm-up songs pros love," or "favorite recovery foods of pros" type of articles—I will almost never spend more than a few minutes trying to find contact info for a racer. So if you want to become a popular go-to resource for journalists, put yourself out there!

Another mistake racers do make is abandoning a page and not updating it occasionally. Check in on it to make sure links are still working and race results are being updated at least a few times in a season, and always make sure that your contact info is correct. If you decide to stop updating or you don't want to have a page anymore for whatever reason, delete it or set up a redirect to your best social page. Don't just leave it sitting dormant.

Again, this doesn't mean you need to blog or do regular updates, it just means your page should always list your current team, social media handles, and contact info. You don't need more than a single page, if you want to keep it simple.

Add widgets that auto-update: If you have a Twitter or Instagram feed, you can add a widget to the side of your site that pulls in those updates. It's a great/easy way to keep your site seeming current while not needing to spend a lot of time on it.

In many ways, an influencer will not have the same credibility as an athlete when it comes to certain types of advice, so if that's your lane, make sure you stay aware of how you're talking to your audience.

Athlete's content supports the training and racing journey and also gives tips to the followers in the process. Influencer's content may be different because it may only be about pretty pictures or looking good next to the bike. That's shifting more and more as athlete/influencer begins to blend, but it's just a good thing to be aware of as you're creating content.

Want to add content but not sure what to add?
—Race reports
—Links to results/articles that you're featured or mentioned in
—Your favorite pieces of gear and how you use them
—Training tips or healthy recipes
—Team announcements, your race schedule, upcoming events

I recommend that if you're starting this site to be your ATHLETE focused page, you stick to writing about sport-related content. This can involve stuff that's somewhat related, it doesn't have to be all race-focused—your favorite books on the sport, a great recipe for a healthy dinner, that kind of stuff is great. But talking about your trip to comic con, for example, clouds the message you're trying to get across. There are some exceptions, a few racers who manage to have info about other hobbies on their sites, but for the most part, it's not a great idea, unless it's something you're super-passionate about and really want to blend into your career.

Add photos! Hey, remember that photoshoot we just talked about? This is a great place to put some of those images! Lastly, make sure your site is linked to in all of your social media channels.

Get going: If you already have a website, go check it and make sure info is up to date, and that your site looks clean. If you don't have a site and want one, head to wordpress.com and set up a free site. You can go premium and get that domain later if you want, but for now, I'm a fan of starting with the free option and going crazy once you've started actually using it regularly. For now, play around.

BUSINESS OF FITNESS

Keeping Your $hit Tight: Helpful Apps

So, in addition to game day, the other place you want to keep your $hit tight is in your organization. That means your emails, messaging, expenses and travel. I've seen a few contracts not get renewed because someone kept missing flights because she was so unorganized. Don't be like that. Flaky is for amateurs.

It's tempting to end up with dozens of helpful apps that you read about in a '10 apps to help you save time' article, but honestly, after working as a team manager running travel, expenses, social media and sponsorship connections, I quickly found that less is more. These are the the categories that I found needed tracking as a pro, a team manager, or an influencer—obviously, you may find one category isn't important to you, i.e if you don't travel for work, you can skip the travel category. The apps that you personally like will vary, but here's what I've found works for each category and how I use each.

Organizer
Google Sheets FTW. I had one main sheet to coordinate a season for three racers, three mechanics and myself. The main page was a list of races with all of the relevant info for the team on the season overall. Then, each race had its own tab, with all the travel/flight/driving info for each racer and team staffer, plus a timetable for the weekend. There were also tabs for keeping track of sponsorship info and things like that. It's amazing how much you can do in a single sheet—and you can set it to be available offline!

Expense Tracker
QuickBooks is great if you're planning to deduct expenses from taxes (and you should), since it helps you both keep track of your finances as well as

send invoices and even accept payments. If you're a serious athlete/influencer in it for the long haul, this is the smart way to keep track of everything. If you're just getting into it, though, a less intensive, free option is Mint for expense tracking and recording.

Smart Email
Spark is great for your phone because you can delay messages in your inbox and have them bounce back to you at appropriate times. It also has a 'Smart Inbox' feature so it predicts which emails are important and which are spam types, making it ideal for someone who's bad at keeping up with his or her inbox.

Travel Planner
While I prefer using a combo of Google Sheets and Google Calendar, a lot of racers I know prefer TripIt to keep track of all of their flights and hotels. It syncs with your email and you can add multiple people to a trip, making it ideal for simplifying when you need to be at the airport. (But I personally prefer my travel info to be in my calendar since it's part of my day-to-day, so I prefer to stick with Google Calendar.)

Social Media Scheduler
Buffer is a cheap, easy way to space out your posts so you don't spend all day on social media—instead, you can batch it as a once-a-week chore to get your basic posts done, then add fun and spontaneous ones throughout the week. Really, scheduling allows you more time to be creative.

To Do List
Google Calendars is so feature-rich that most racers and influencers can live by it. It's also the most convenient when you're consistently making plans/meetings with other people, since you can share events and invite people to attend calls/meetings/trips.

Create An "ALWAYS ANSWER" Contact List

This sounds like a small thing, but the bigger you get, the harder it is to stay on top of your communications. I've watched a few racers and influencers miss out on great opportunities, paid work, new sponsors, and fun events because they couldn't stay on top of their inbox. Which, fair enough, can be tough to do for anyone.

That's why it's important to create a list of people that you always respond to promptly. Make your ALWAYS ANSWER list include both personal and professional contacts. Think about people who can make or break your career if they don't hear from you.

This might include:
-Your team manager
-Your agent
-The press officer at the company sponsoring you this season
-The assistant in charge of sending you gear from a sponsor
-An editor at a magazine who always includes you in stories
-Your parents (like I said, don't forget the personal in here!)
-Your BFF (I've seen a lot of friendships break down because an athlete just let his or her inbox/texts/voicemails overflow and missed important moments with friends)

Keep this list as short as you can make it. Once you have this ALWAYS ANSWER list, you can keep it somewhere easy to spot to remind you of how you should prioritize your responses. Alternatively, you can even get fancier with email app plugins, setting up a folder that filters these emails, making that folder the one you check every single day, and saving the rest of your inbox for later. On your phone, you can set notifications for specific emails.

I'm a firm believer in checking email/messages/texts at least once a day and responding to as much as possible. Weekly, I try to zero out my inboxes—and that doesn't mean that I respond to everything, but it does mean everything is read and everything that needs to be responded to is responded to.

This ALWAYS ANSWER list is just a starting point, since as you grow, you'll be adding more names to this list, but if you know you're not the best communicator / you tend to leave your inbox piling up, this is a good place to begin.

Forming Your Own Team

Whether you're an influencer or an athlete, going it alone can be ... well, lonely. Forming a crew can help boost you on social media channels as you support each other, boost results if you're more athlete-focused, and can potentially be a lot more fun and fulfilling than trying to go it alone.

Think *collective* **versus** *team*
Especially when you're new at the whole team-building thing, a healthier way to think of it might be the collective approach: You're sharing, you're supporting each other, but there's no one leader calling the shots. You can even consider forming a looser collective where everyone can keep individual sponsors/exist outside of the group as solopreneurs, but you agree to collaborate on certain projects (or for racers, agree to work together at races, both in the race itself but also in getting team tent space, sharing a mechanic, etc.).

Know what you want
Depending on how you structure your team, you may be essentially running a small business, so understand what you're committing to. Are you hoping to create a team that actually will have support, like a team manager and coach? If you're a business-oriented person, like a yoga instructor, the similar question to ask is are you hoping to run a studio that would involve having a staff like a receptionist, et cetera, or are you hoping to find another couple of teachers to go in on renting a room at a local gym or studio together and pooling classes and clients? Before you start asking your friends to join your crew, think about what you're asking for: will they be buying in, getting paid, bringing sponsors... Figure that out before

getting everyone excited.

Find like-minded, similarly talented people
This may sound obvious, but if you're planning on forming a crew that thrives, you want like-minded people. If you're wellness influencers, pairing a high-fat carnivore with a raw vegan may not be the best pairing (then again, it might just work!). If you're a racing team, a first-season beginner may not be ideal for a teammate if you're a 10-year veteran of the sport and winning races, even if you're best friends outside of racing.

(And consider personalities)
Not to be a total downer, but you need to think about the vibe of your team that you're hoping to form. People who are best friends IRL may not make for the best team/work partners—you may end up with competitive vibes that didn't exist before.

Pool sponsors and resources
If person #1 has a clothing sponsor, person #2 has a nutritional supplement sponsor and person #3 has a shoe sponsor, if you can get all of those sponsors together, you end up with a pretty legitimate setup.

And have a sponsor plan
The tricky thing with teams is when everyone starts emailing the sponsors about individual needs, random questions and honestly, even thank yous. It can get overwhelming to sponsors, and it makes a group of people harder to work with. Each sponsor should have a designated point person, whether that means one person in your new crew becomes the point person for dealing with sponsors on the whole, or each person has one or two sponsors that they specifically handle.

Ensure sponsors are taken care of
You don't need to be the enforcer, but you should make sure everyone is on board with doing his or her part to make a sponsor happy. Send out an email to the teammates that you've brought on highlighting what you expect them to post on social media about the team, and any do's and don'ts, plus all race obligations.

Stay organized
Spreadsheets will become your best friend if you're going to wade into the waters of teaming up with other athletes or influencers. Knowing where

money is coming from and where it's going can be a huge headache, as can knowing what each of you is expected to do for sponsors, your race calendar and travel schedule, et cetera. (Google Sheets is great for this since everyone on the team can have access.)

Know what you're getting into

I've seen A LOT of athletes try to start their own teams, and to be honest, it rarely goes well. That's because a lot of athletes accidentally start trying to run their own teams versus forming that more loosely structured collective concept. Soon, the athlete who started the whole thing has gone from being an athlete to being more of a manager, and often the original point of the formation of the group—to help pool resources and give you a leg up in your field—has disappeared and all you're doing is supporting other athletes in ways that you had hoped to be supported yourself. So be clear going in about what you ARE willing to do—be the point man talking to sponsors, for example—and what you're NOT on the hook for, like booking flights to competitions.

Should You Try Personal Fundraising?

Fundraising might sound like a thing that your high school band would do to go to State Championships or something, but what if you look at fundraising as 'crowdsourcing small-scale sponsorships'?

Essentially, fundraising is asking your friends/family/community to sponsor you. With that in mind, there are a couple of things you should do:

Start by remembering that you're asking people with normal 9-to-5 jobs to help you live your dream. Keep that in mind, always.

Have a reason. What are you asking for and why? For an athlete, you might be looking for money to fund travel for a racing season.

Have a goal in mind. As we talked about with budget spreadsheets, you need to know what your ask is, and be prepared to explain it: break down the cost of flights/whatever it is that you're doing.

Have a 'give.' What are people getting for free from you? This is more influencer-focused: If all you're doing is posting IG photos, your Patreon or Kickstarter is unlikely to get funded. If you have a series of instructional yoga videos that people are already watching and using, that's content that they're already getting for free. Make sure you have something like that in place—a GIVE—before you make an ASK. It doesn't need to be much.

Set up a way to donate. Use a site like Patreon, Kickstarter or any of the other sites like that. That way, it's easy to track and keeps your accounting pretty simple (versus taking cash and the potential tax/bookkeeping nightmares that can come with that).

Create a set of bonuses. Maybe that means sending a signed jersey for donations of over $500, or a signed poster, or a water bottle, et cetera. (Your sponsors might even be able to give you some swag for giveaways.)

Don't be pushy. Fundraising is very hit-or-miss, and can turn some people off (more on that in a second). Use all of your social channels, send out a mass email, but then, don't keep emailing or continue to push it on social media.

While it might be tempting to set up a generic Kickstarter or GoFundMe page to help finance your season, most potential sponsors find the practice a little irritating. Nearly every sponsor or team owner interviewed for this guide said that seeing a rider set one up, especially without a specific need or story behind it, was a turn-off in most circumstances.

There are certainly exceptions, and we'll get into them, but it's a hard sell to ask friends and family for charitable donations to your able-bodied race season when there are so many other organizations advocating for truly needy people throughout the world. So before you set up that page, seriously consider just what you're asking for, why you're asking for it, and what you already have.

If you already have a team, absolutely, positively do not set up any kind of GoFundMe page without talking to your team director or manager beforehand. "It bothers me in a year that I'm working with the athlete, seeing him or her set one up," says one former team manager and sponsorship coordinator at a major bike brand. "It doesn't look professional." He explains that's because it suggests that your team isn't providing you with adequate support, and it makes them look bad. If you set up a fundraising site, you're basically saying that you're not getting paid enough—and for your team, that can be embarrassing, whether or not it's accurate. If you get the OK from your team, that's fine. If you don't, but you still need to raise money to get by, email a smaller group of supporters or approach individuals versus starting a web-based fundraiser.

If you're self-funding your whole season, you might be able to get away with starting a GoFundMe page, but tread carefully. Again, remember: You're asking people who are working 40 hour weeks, probably more, to fund your life. For some people, this can feel a bit distasteful, when there are so many worthy causes that they could be donating to. So before you do make that ask, honestly ask yourself if there's another way you can raise capital (i.e. selling some old gear or getting a part-time job).

If you really think this is your best option, go ahead and build a page, but make sure you get clear about what the money will be funding (even posting your race schedule), offer plenty of personality and fun details and photos, and try to figure out a way to give back to those who help you out.

"If a rider does that for one season—gets themselves to major races domestic and abroad—they should get the attention they need to have a real sponsorship the following season," says one marketer. "That's good story. I think it is completely reasonable for an unknown to take that route."

If you're trying to raise money for a specific event, again, it's important to check first with your team and governing body before asking the Internet for cash donations. It's reasonable to ask friends and family for help, but again, be clear on what you're asking for, provide details about costs (people don't often know how expensive it is for riders to race for their countries!), and offer fun prizes for donating.

If you decide to set up a page, think about it the same way you would your personal website or your Twitter page: use great pictures, proofread your prose, and provide thoughtful, interesting details and information. No one wants to donate to a page that's poorly setup and badly written!

And, of course, don't forget to send thank you notes—via snail mail, not email.

Get Everything in Writing

It's tempting to take a new potential sponsor at his word, or assume that a new teammate on the team you're forming will definitely live up to expectations. But unfortunately, that isn't always the world we live in. As the kids say, get receipts.

A lot of smaller teams and sponsors won't bother with a racer contract, since often they're also operating on a shoestring budget and don't have extra cash for lawyers. This is where things can get dicey, so it's always smart to follow up any conversations had in person or over the phone with an email that you can refer to later.

Have those great conversations with a potential new sponsor at a race… And then go home and email that person with a quick summary of what you discussed.

Chat on the phone with your new team manager about what bikes you'll be riding this season, and follow up with an email outlining what you discussed.

When chatting with a new sponsor about your social media obligations, list them out and send them back in an email to clarify.

Basically, always create a paper trail, so that if a situation arises where you find yourself needing to defend a choice you made or ask for what you were promised, you have written and time-stamped proof.

A Few Reminders About Contracts

When you're negotiating or renegotiating a contract, remember that you're starting from zero every time. Even if you've been with a company for a decade, you're still subject to the way the company has performed over the past couple years, the direction that the company is taking, the people who've come and gone—so much is subject to change. The worst thing that a sponsored athlete can do is get too comfortable and assume that every renegotiation will be at worst, a contract for the same amounts of stuff and cash, or at best, a huge raise.

Many pros will tell you contract horror stories—last minute changes, sudden company closures. Unfortunately, you're in a volatile space: Not only do your results and what you bring to the table matter, you're also at the mercy of the landscape of that particular sport. In the early 1990s, there was serious cash in cross-country mountain bike racing. Now, it's harder than ever to get a decent sponsor and team setup, even for the highest-level riders.

When companies start to struggle, one of the first things that can go is the sponsorship dollars—for many sports companies, the advertising return on investment for sponsored athletes rarely is what's raking in the big bucks, so it's an easy way to cut costs without making any internal cuts.

So all of this to say, stay humble. As one pro reminded me, approach each sponsorship negotiation hopeful, but remember that you're not guaranteed to make what you've been making or more—every time you negotiate, you're technically starting from zero. While it's not the most optimistic approach, it's a good dose of reality that might help you avoid writing checks you can't cash throughout the year, or coming to the bargaining table with a serious chip on your shoulder about what you think you deserve.

"Sponsorship is only partially related to what you're doing and bringing to the table as an athlete," one long-time pro warns. "At the end of the day, you're a line item in a budget, and could always get cut."

And lastly, as one pro warns, if you sign a contract, make sure you get a countersigned copy and you keep that copy for your records. A lot of times a brand will send you the contract to sign and you send it back (but they haven't signed it yet). Make sure you ask for the counter-signed copy after returning it with your signature, otherwise, legally there won't be much you can do if they backtrack on their promises later. If the sponsor doesn't send a contract, simply write up an email describing what you've agreed to and send it, asking them to confirm the sponsorship description. It may not be legally binding, but it will give you a handy point of reference if you run into any disputes or if the company hires new sponsorship coordinators.

Curating Your Personal Team

If you're reading this, I'm guessing you're not in a position to hire a manager, an agent, an accountant or a lawyer to help you out. But there are a few people you can add to your posse instead, or pay on an hourly basis.

An older pro still in your field
Ideally, this person would still be active in your sport, would have achieved a good amount, and was or is on a team that you admire. You might not get the top guy in the sport to sit down with you and chat, but there are likely plenty of pros who would be willing to hop on a quick call and offer you advice or listen to your various offers and opportunities and weigh in.

A retired pro who has a life you want
This person will likely be a bit more cynical and can help push you in a direction that will benefit you long after you're done racing. He or she should be someone savvy that you can honestly run contracts and offers by, and know that he or she will be able to advise you to sign a contract or negotiate harder. A retired pro is ideal here because a racer who's still competing may not always have your best interests at heart.

A coach
There are plenty of coaches who aren't super expensive and having a coach is great for both your training and for talking through opportunities as well as helping with things like letters of recommendation for teams and sponsors. Even if you're not working with a coach on a daily basis, having someone oversee your training and development can be a huge help. Teams and sponsors often look for racers who work with coaches because it shows a certain level of commitment, and for young riders, often a coach's recommendation is mandatory for getting into a national-level camp. Many coaches will offer free or extremely cheap consults if you just

want someone to look over your current training (and if you do work with a coach now but are wondering why you're not progressing the way you hope, it might be worth consulting with another coach!).

A friend outside of the sport
You know your cynical friend who never comes to a race, who works a 9 to 5 and regularly contributes to his 401K? He is a great sounding-board for sharing your options and plans, and seeing how they would play out in the real world. Sure, it's hard for him to understand exactly where you're coming from, but it's a good idea to make sure you maintain friendships outside of your sport for your mental health as well as to see what life beyond racing looks like.

A friend in a similar position to you
A big issue I see a lot in sport is that athletes rarely discuss money with each other. I think it's largely because it's a matter of pride: no one wants to admit what they're making because they worry it's lower than what someone else is getting. But... If we don't talk to other people about what we're making, we may never know what the 'asking rate' actually is, and we run a risk of all of us being undercut. So find someone who's getting similar results to you and offer to compare notes. It's a great way to stay in touch with what's really happening in your sport. (If you can gather a few of these friends and be honest with each other—and vow to not try to steal sponsors from each other—that's even better.) Knowledge is power, people!

An accountant
Many of them will have an hourly fee, and occasional appointments to talk finances can be invaluable, especially early on as you're establishing yourself. As an athlete, you're a business, not just a person, so you need to treat your money like a business would.

A lawyer
Again, most will have hourly rates and if you have a contract in hand that's offering real, bill-paying money, it's worth having a lawyer look it over and make sure everything looks OK and you won't be selling your soul. (Consider this: a lawyer will likely take around $200 / hour, so if you're holding a contract for $10,000, isn't $200 worth it to make sure you can maximize that?)

When Saying YES to the Contract

Remember, just because a contract is in front of you doesn't mean you've agreed to it. Or that you have to.

"The bigger the brand, the more the money," adds one sponsorship coordinator. "But just because it's big, don't expect a ton of spending in every area—a lot of the biggest companies don't have cyclocross budgets. And you have multiple resources, multiple demands, more sophisticated contracts. A smaller brand, they make it up as they go along. Much more of a family, a little less dialed. Every dollar counts. And that's not a bad thing."

It's time to read the fine print. And it's time to be willing to negotiate.

A few things to consider:

Salary versus one-time payment versus bonus structure
There isn't a best answer here, but it is important to know what the usual options are. Bonus structures are the riskiest but most common—always make sure you can afford to live even if your season goes terribly. "My preference with cash is to base it heavily on results through a bonus structure," one manager says. "Remember you as an athlete—'Talent' is the tongue-in-cheek but accurate term—deal directly with the marketing manager, and he has to continually sell you to his own managers. Your contact with the brand has to justify you as a line in the budget every day."

Food or travel stipends
Make sure you're clear on exactly how the company wants this accounted for: Do they need receipts on Monday right after the race if you're going to be reimbursed? Is there a maximum? Do they want you to book flights

on your credit card or will they?

Gear ownership

At the end of the season, do you own that race bike or those eight pairs of unworn running shoes? If so, are there any stipulations about resale? A lot of athletes can actually add a hefty amount to their salary by selling off gently used or still-new gear at the end of the season, but some teams sneak in a clause about getting all of their gear back at the end of the year so they can sell it and recoup some cash.

Who decides your race schedule?

What happens if there's a dispute between a race you want to do and what the team wants you to do? Make sure it's spelled out so when these arguments come up, you know what your options are.

What do they want you to do?

Read this very carefully, and don't commit unless you're absolutely willing to do every single thing that they've laid out.

Ask someone else to read the contract

Before you sign, ask a lawyer/friend/coach/parent/any trustworthy party to look it over. They might catch clauses that you missed that raise a red flag.

Get it counter-signed

I mentioned it before but remember, just because you signed the contract, until you get a copy back signed by the sponsor, it's not a valid contract. So make sure you ask for the counter-signed copy and save it.

Think Laterally About Money

Sponsorship dollars are just one piece of the pie for most racers who are making it in the sport. Sure, the top guys who are winning the Tour de France are doing pretty well, but even most runners who place top 5 in the Boston Marathon or another major race are likely earning money some other way in addition to their running.

It's time to think creatively about how you're making money.

A few ways I've seen racers make extra cash:

Keeping an eye on prize money
Even some local races can have decent prize purses, especially if you can work with the promoter to get free race entry. A couple hundred dollars can mean the difference between shopping at Whole Foods or eating ramen noodles all month.

Selling your old gear
Try not to let your gear languish in your parent's garage for long. The longer it sits, the less value it holds, so regularly sell your old gear (not your old running shoes, obviously, think things like bikes and barely used clothing) online with sites like Poshmark or by sending it to a resale spot like Protested Gear (for cyclists).

Making tshirts/other gear
There are plenty of ways now to create and sell your own tshirts, cycling socks, bags... the list goes on and on. This isn't going to be lucrative right from the start, but it's certainly a channel you can consider trying out. It's especially useful when doing a specific fundraising effort with limited-run

sales, since people are more likely to support you when there's some kind of bonus in it for them..

Piecemeal work

There are plenty of simple side hustles you can do even with a travel and training schedule that doesn't leave you room for a normal 9 to 5. You can pick up dog-walking jobs with an app like Rover, or let your former boss know that you have some availability to pick up shifts, or simply ask local sponsors if they have any work you can do. You'd be surprised how many low-commitment ways there are to make a few bucks if you look.

Being smart with spending

If you can save money, that's money you don't need to earn. A few no-impact, no-stress ways:

Booking at the right time

When planning your flights, the best rule of thumb is to book around 5 to 6 weeks before your event. I've known a lot of racers who waiting until the last minute and got stuck with the worst flight times and terrible prices because they weren't planning ahead. The same applies to hotels in busy areas.

Credit card programs

I know a lot of racers who manage to use credit cards with travel points or cash-back programs in such smart ways that they're able to cover flights, hotels and more with their points.

Frequent flyer programs

Same goes, especially if you're traveling a lot by air. Some frequent flyer programs won't cover flight costs but will defray expenses by giving you free checked baggage. Saving even $50 per flight can add up to a lot over the course of a season!

Rebate programs

There are great online plugins that automatically get you cash back when you shop online. Some of the rewards are minimal, but some give you even 15% off of purchases, which can be huge if you're booking a week in a hotel for $1000.

Travel discount sites
Speaking of hotels, hotels.com offers 1 night free for every 10 nights of booked hotels—this adds up to a couple free nights per season which, again, adds up over the season. Other travel sites have similar deals, so look for what works best for you.

Trip alerts
Google Flights has a simple flight-tracking feature to help you figure out the cheapest time to book. Being smart about when you book can save you thousands over the course of the season.

Fly smart
For sports that involve a lot of equipment, like cycling, know what airlines charge for flying with your bike. You may realize that while a ticket with an airline is the cheapest, their bike fees can add $500 to the cost of your roundtrip ticket. Meanwhile, an airline with a pricier roundtrip ticket might only change $100 per bike flight.

Eat smarter
Food on the road adds up quite a bit, so the thriftiest racers get creative about bringing things like a kettle and a rice cooker with them so that they can make their own simple but tasty meals in hotel rooms easily.

Bigger payoffs
And a few ways that require a bit more work and education, but can be long-term career solutions afterwards:

Getting a job
You won't be the first professional rider to work a full-time job—plenty of Olympic athletes work traditional office jobs. In some cases, those athletes actually did better while working full-time and racing, because they were less stressed about their results and if sponsors were happy. Alternatively, a 20-hour week working at a running shop or bike shop might be enough to cover living expenses while you focus on your athletic career.

Hosting camps and clinics
Again, this is a huge level of commitment, but hosting a clinic or a camp for the sport that you're an expert in can be a great side hustle. It's ideal if

you team up with someone who has coaching/planning expertise, though, and start small. A half-day clinic is a good starting point: Don't start with a week-long camp in a location you don't know well! Partnering with a local club or shop for this can be an easy way to make new connections as well.

Coaching

I know quite a few racers who've sought the extra education needed to pursue part time coaching (that transitioned into full time coaching when they were done with their careers). If you're interested in coaching, consider seeking a coach willing to mentor you rather than setting up a business on your own.

Journalism

There are some bigger examples like New York Times-Bestselling author and ultra-runner Scott Jurek, but on a smaller scale, that column that you've been writing for a magazine for free could turn into a paid regular feature. Don't be afraid to ask, the worst you'll hear is, 'No, we can't pay you.'

Remember though: if you want to be a professional athlete, that comes first. It's easy to accidentally fall into the 'I need more money, I need to work more' trap, but refer back to that budget you made earlier in this book. Money is great, it's important, but if you're serious about being an athlete, it's not the thing you should be focused on beyond making enough to live. If you want to make a ton of cash, go to school and become a lawyer.

What To Do Next

If you read this all at once, your head is probably spinning right now. There's so much to do and so much to think about. You need to revamp your athlete resume while building a new website, rethinking your social media, planning a race season, emailing new potential teams and sponsors… and somehow do all of that on top of school or work plus the hours you need to actually spend training.

It probably feels like too much. And if you try to tackle everything at once, it absolutely is too much for one person to take on in a single weekend. But slowly implemented, these tools we've gone through can help you make the most of your talent for whatever sport you're in. And you're never too old or too young to get started on setting up for success in your athletic career.

So, what the heck are you supposed to do next? It depends where you are in your season. If you're smack-dab in race season, it might be time to focus on those race-day specific tips and improving your social media game. If you're wrapping up a season, it might be time to work on polishing your athlete resume and updating your website while sending a few thank you notes.

Don't be afraid to start small: Whether it's a local gym giving you a few free hours of massage therapy or personal training, or a bike shop that's willing to give you a bike for the season, or a company willing to give you frequent flyer miles to get to races, those small things can add up to major wins, and can lead to bigger, better and more lucrative deals. Red Bull probably isn't going to come knocking on your door, but a local kombucha brewer might be willing to help you out.

Remember: Be kind, be yourself, work hard and be humble, and you're going to be great.

Keep Learning

To stay informed with more information, tools and resources, check out AthleteSponsorshipGuide.com

On the site, we'll have:
-Templates for race resumes
-Links to great interviews and tips from pros who've been there, done that
-Lists of the best athletes to follow to see how to crush it at social media
-Interviews with young racers who've made their way onto great teams and sponsorship programs
-Interviews with more sponsorship coordinators
-Tons of freebies and articles that will keep you up-to-date on the best practices as the world of sport and sponsorship keeps evolving!

About the Author

Take a deep breath, because the list of what Molly Hurford is up to takes a minute to get through. Molly has built her career with several aims in mind: Write constantly, race often, travel frequently and live on her own terms, mostly outside. While she runs her own brands, including The Outdoor Edit, The Consummate Athlete Podcast and Shred Girls, she also works as a freelance writer for many major outdoor publications. (She's been called one of the most connected reporters in cycling, and is one of the first freelance female cycling journalists—and one of the few who's refused to make a 9 to 5 shift.)

She's also a cycling coach and yoga teacher, and obsessed with getting more women psyched on adventure and wellness. She regularly hosts talks and coaches clinics and camps for cyclists. She teaches yoga when she is home, and when she isn't, she's often recording new yoga videos for The Ryan Leech Connection or TheOutdoorEdit.com.

She's also the author of multiple books on cycling and nutrition. Her most recent project, Shred Girls, is a young adult fiction series focused on getting girls excited about bikes. It's also a website that features interviews, advice and inspiration for young female cyclists at Shred-Girls.com.

Her earlier works included 'Fuel Your Ride' and 'Saddle, Sore: Ride Comfortable, Ride Happy.' She also writes regularly for publications including Bicycling magazine, Outside, Map My Run, and Nylon.

In her spare time, Molly has raced almost every type of bike, from cyclocross to road to mountain at an elite level; competed in triathlons from sprint to Ironman; and currently spends most of her time competing in ultra-running races.

You can find out more about her, her speaking and coaching, and her books at TheOutdoorEdit.com

Made in the USA
Monee, IL
28 September 2020

43474841R00106